Jeanette Han [...] 1955. She emi[...] in 1981, where she now lives. She enjoys inspirational (in spirit) writing, astrology and mythology. A life threatening illness in 1992 renewed her love of inspirational writing, which resulted in the publication of some of her poetry. This 'second chance' at life deepened her spiritual awareness, inviting her to follow a new direction.

Ann Ann, also known as 'Ann Ann the Extraordinaire', one of Australia's most respected psychics and clairvoyants, has worked in the public domain using her abilities for many years. She has held regular guest spots on Austereo radio programmes throughout Australia and has had her own national programme. Ann has also appeared as a guest on television programmes such as *In Melbourne Tonight (IMT)*, *The Denise Show* and *A Current Affair*. A seasoned event speaker who has toured around the country, Ann has conducted seminars both in Australia and the US and has hosted radio programmes there.

DEATH
OF A
PRINCE

Jack the Ripper and Other Souls

JEANETTE HAN
with ANN ANN

ARROW

An Arrow Book
Published by
Random House Australia Pty Ltd
20 Alfred Street, Milsons Point, NSW 2061
http://www.randomhouse.com.au

Sydney   New York   Toronto
London   Auckland   Johannesburg

First published 2001

National Library of Australia
Cataloguing-in-Publication Entry

Han, Jeanette
Death of a prince: Jack the Ripper and other souls

Bibliography

ISBN 1 74 051062 3

1. Jack, the Ripper. 2. Parapsychology – England – London.
3. Psychics – England – London. I. Ann, Ann. II. Title.

133.809421

Extract from
'The Wine is Drunk',
Gwen Harwood, *Selected Poems*
(Angus & Robertson, 1975),
used by permission.

Cover photograph by IPL Pro~File
Internal design by Midland Typesetters
Typeset in 12 pt Sabon by Midland Typesetters, Maryborough, Victoria
Printed and bound by Griffin Press, Netley, South Australia

10 9 8 7 6 5 4 3 2 1

To the person I once was.
To the life I once had.

Jeanette Han

Contents

Acknowledgements

'I must in this gross darkness cherish
more than all plenitude the hunger
that drives the spirit.'

'The Wine is Drunk'
Selected Poems
Gwen Harwood

We thank spirit for their gift of vision. To this end, we give gratitude to all those who made this 'journey of the soul' possible.

The physical journey was made manifest with the help of two women. Renee Richter and Deborah Marsland from Harvey World Travel, Queensland said that when they organised this 'one-off' trip they were 'just doing their job'. It was more than that. It was an act of kindness that helped many souls.

We also wish to thank Bronwyn Marquardt who describes herself as a freelance journalist. She is an emissary of light. It was through her efforts that this book found its way onto the publisher's desk. Thank you, all.

1

Ashfield, Sydney 1988

'There is talk he was Jack the Ripper you know.' I whispered these words to someone sitting behind me in the small sandstone chapel. It was the late 1800s and I was wearing a charcoal grey dress with a cream lace collar. The collar was stiff and made my neck itch as I turned to talk to whoever sat behind me. I remember thinking to myself that I was brought here to marry him, Prince Eddy. Instead, I'm at his funeral. Yet, I couldn't ignore the exhilaration I felt. It didn't matter. I would marry his brother.

* * *

Ann Ann expressed the above recollection during a past-life meditation with a therapist in Ashfield,

Sydney in the late 1980s. She gave her name as Princess May of Teck and said it in a guttural tone. Earlier in the therapy, Ann described a childhood scene. She was in beautiful, cool countryside with lush, uncut grass. The sun touched her skin as she watched children playing in the distance, however she knew that she was not a part of the family.

As Princess May of Teck, Ann heard the other children's laughter and watched their nannies play with them. They were all under five years of age and were beautifully dressed. When the therapist asked Ann a question, she tried to answer, but was unable to bring the words forward. She could understand English, but could not speak it. She knew she was German.

After this event, Ann, known in Australia as the psychic Ann Ann Extraordinaire, did some research to find out if there ever had been a Princess May of Teck. Her findings astounded her. She had indeed linked into a past life and experienced the feelings of the woman who would become the British Monarchy's Queen Mary.

Ann was overwhelmed by the whole event and was unsure why it had happened. It was to be some ten years later before there was a reconnection to that day. Whilst reading a weekend newspaper, Ann noticed an advertisement for a tour of British castles. She felt that it would be more interesting if there was a psychic picking up extra information guiding the tourists.

The following Monday, Ann phoned Harvey World Travel, Queensland to discuss the idea of a psychic tour. The woman she spoke to was keen to explore it and rang back later that day. She told Ann to pencil in a tentative trip for the latter part of the year, and said she would present it at the next company meeting for discussion. Well, the idea was accepted and Ann was the first person in Australia to provide an overseas psychic tour for her radio and television followers. The package included learning about psychic development so that the participants could utilise their intuitive abilities. And so it was through this embryo of an idea that the birth of many new and exciting discoveries took place.

2

How It All Began

11 October 1998

Our journey was to be extraordinary. No one on the trip knew just how strange this adventure would be. I flew from Perth, Western Australia to Brisbane, Queensland. It was my intention to soak up the city's atmosphere before joining the others on the first leg of the trip. The first person who approached me at Brisbane airport was Karen. She guessed that I was one of the people on the tour, and we chatted for a while until it was time to board the aircraft. Ann arrived and introduced herself to us, and she was the only other person we met up with at Brisbane airport. Our flight took off for Hong Kong where we would meet the other members of the group. Karen and Ann sat together on one side and I had a window seat opposite them.

I watched the fields, lined and green, become smaller as the plane climbed higher towards the summer sun, and its wing cast a shadow over the ever-diminishing land below. As we flew over the South Pacific Ocean, I was enchanted by the vibrancy of its colour. The vivid blue water barely rippled, and it sharply contrasted the green oasis land that it surrounded. White-edged deltas reflected the brilliance of the Australian sunshine, and rippled veins of sand snaked through the iridescent water. We crossed the Artesian Basin and I had to peer through the mottled, shadowy clouds until finally we had climbed so high that it felt as though I was looking down on the sky. Despite being an adult experiencing this in the Southern Hemisphere, it reminded me of my childhood in Scotland. I was about ten years old and had gone out for a ride on my new bicycle. It was summer, and I remember how I soaked in the peace of that day taking notice of everything around me. A child's inner world can be beautiful, and the beginning of this journey would lead me back to my homeland where beauty and memories would meet like old friends.

* * *

We all came from different states in Australia and met at Hong Kong airport. We gathered together, rather nervously at first, and began introducing ourselves and telling each other which part of Australia we had come from. But, more importantly, we wanted to know why each one of us had fought so hard to be a part of the psychic tour. It became clear that some had struggled to get the finances together, whilst others had worked hard to convince their partners that they simply had to experience this journey. Whatever the difficulties, we all understood that the trip was vital to our souls. Excitement began to build as we chatted about the many nights we'd spent listening to Ann Ann on the radio and the avid listeners' responses as she gave them information on their lives and hope for the future.

I understood how these callers felt, because in March 1998 I was one of the callers Ann had contacted in Perth to link with radio station B105 in Brisbane. I had written a letter to the station to ask about details of the tour. About two weeks later I was just waking up from a vision of a tarot card. The card was the Page of Wands. It seemed as though I had seen this card flashing before my eyes all night. The Page of Wands is all about an exciting message, the beginning of an adventure. I then woke up to the sound of the telephone ringing. It was 6:00am.

'Hi! This is Ann Ann here from Brisbane.'

I was truly shocked and couldn't contain my excitement. She went on to say that she wanted to do a reading for me on air, and she would like me to have my tarot cards by the phone as she would use them just for something different. What was even more of a revelation was that Ann said she received approximately 700 letters a week and only picked out five or six for readings.

So, our connection was no coincidence. That night on the radio, Ann told me a few things and one was that I would be writing a book, although it was some way down the track. Seven months later when the trip began, Ann understandably couldn't remember the reading she had given me. What was unusual however, was that she asked me if I would like to write a book about the sequential events of the tour.

There were many personal problems for us both over the following year, but we surmounted them and our vision was recaptured in October 1999. What you are about to read is a record of our experiences on the psychic tour, how each person was affected, and the subsequent shocking discovery relating to the Jack-the-Ripper mystery.

3

Jack the Ripper

12 October 1998

It was a clear, sunny October morning when we
arrived in London. Two people from Western
Australia still hadn't arrived. Ron and Linda had
not appeared and eventually we had to leave
Heathrow airport without them. After we checked
in to the Tower Hotel Ann came up to my room
for a cup of tea and a chat. We stood at the window
and looked out on to the harbour. Ann began
talking about the importance of our surroundings.

'Always take in the symbolism of what's around
you. It's like a picture of your life to come. If you
can take notice of these things, then make the
effort to write them down. You'll be surprised at
the accuracy of events.'

The harbour was indeed a 'safe' harbour, but

the water appeared stagnant and murky. Three beautiful yachts rocked silently in their moorings. The largest vessel's flag was flying in the breeze. Other flags were hanging around the harbour's edge. They had the letter 'H' on them.

'You might find that the "H" means something to you,' Ann said.

Within six months I had left my twenty-three year marriage and gone back to my maiden name of 'Han'. I would never have anticipated this major, life-changing event. The stagnant water was a clear symbol of my own feelings at that time. There was so much more that I wanted to do with my life, yet I felt that I was unable to express exactly what it was that my soul needed.

Ann continued talking about symbolism and the fact that we were in the Tower Hotel.

'The Tower in tarot cards is all about a sudden, shocking experience. It can mean a murder too.'

We discussed how it also signified enlightenment.

'My room faces the Tower Bridge,' she said. 'It looks glorious lit up in its brilliant blue. I see it as a strong and enduring structure . . . a pathway to the other side.'

The Tower was where our journey began, and all its hidden meanings were to be revealed on our three-week journey through the UK.

When Ann left, I decided to shower and settle down to meditate before we all got together again later that evening. In my meditations I was using the word 'scribe'. Curiously, as I meditated this changed to 'sea-scribe' in my mind. I didn't know why, but I knew it would have some importance later. I took a note of it and joined the rest of the group in the lobby for our first night in London.

* * *

It was nightfall, and the twilight was grey and haunting. Saying goodbye to sunlight and welcoming the dark is a slow process in Britain. The River Thames was like an intimate friend amongst the grand architecture of this old city. We walked along the river on the cobblestone path, hands in pockets discussing where we should go for a meal that night.

As we passed the Tower of London, Ann saw two yeomen standing guard behind the boom gates.

'Millie, would you take a photo of me with the yeomen?'

Ann gave Millie her camera and slipped behind the gate to stand between the two men. She suddenly looked fearful. A man appeared behind her and put his hands under her arms, removing her from the spot.

'You are not supposed to be here!'

She turned and saw a stocky gentleman dressed as Sherlock Holmes. Ann looked quite surprised and told us later that she felt she had been 'caught'. The man in question was a tour guide for 'Ripper Yarns'. He made his apologies, explaining that it was all in good humour.

'Can I interest you ladies in joining our Jack-the-Ripper tour tonight?'

This was an interesting turn of events. Many months before Ann had even thought about a psychic tour, she had mentioned on Australian radio that she was interested in seeing where the Ripper murders took place. Ann often gets a feeling or a hunch that she must follow. Occasionally, the opportunity can manifest itself immediately. But, there are times when she simply must wait until she is inexorably led to something.

Well, this certainly appeared to be the right time with our Sherlock Holmes clone inviting us on the guided tour. Once we'd eaten, we quickly got back to the spot where the tour was to begin. Richard saw us and said he was glad that we could make it.

Gradually, more tourists assembled to join the tour around the very dark streets of Whitechapel where the Jack-the-Ripper murders took place. As we stood in the narrow street where the first murder was committed, Richard told us about the horrifying discovery.

Even though it was 1998, one hundred and ten years after the event, and despite the fact that we were with a group of tourists, the atmosphere was still disquieting. As we huddled together in the chill night air of the dark laneway Richard's voice was a welcome comfort. Yet, there was still a sense of fear in listening to that lone voice talking of the horrendous murders during Queen Victoria's reign.

Our group stayed close together as Richard spoke of one of the Ripper's victims, Martha Tabram. Ann talked to us about the sensations she was getting linked to this incident and asked that we all share any feelings that we 'picked up' about the murder.

'Just go with your first feeling. Don't think! Don't try to analyse anything. Just grasp the feeling. It might be fast and fleeting, but just say what it is.'

I realised that Ann was someone who never questioned her intuition. It was as natural to her as breathing. I noticed that certain people in our group were very intuitive and opened up easily to their feelings. Then, there were some of us who didn't feel confident enough to express ourselves.

But, that would change over the coming days and weeks.

Ann's eyes had a penetrating stare as she spoke about the murder of Martha Tabram.

'She must have been stabbed quite a lot. I can feel these cuts all over my body ... and the blood ... the blood filling up the lungs.'

She shared this insight with Richard who confirmed that her feelings about the way in which Martha Tabram had died were correct. Richard was beginning to look curiously at Ann and asked her what our group was involved in. Ann explained we were all from Australia on a psychic tour. He continued his talk to the group and mentioned that no one knew whether the murderer was right or left-handed.

'The murderer was left-handed,' Ann said.

I watched her eyes flash as she talked of the images and sensations she was getting.

'What makes you say that?' Richard asked.

'Because the incisions were made from behind going right to left. And the head was pushed slightly to one side.'

Richard wanted to know why she felt it had been done this way.

'It was quietly done. The blood flowed down in to the garments. No one would hear anything, and after she was dead they wouldn't see the mess

13

of blood. They would just see a woman sitting propped up on the ground.'

I was amazed at Ann's powers of perception, but she had worked with the police on murder cases in Australia so this was not an unusual experience for her. It was, however, a very unusual experience for Richard. After all, he was leading a group of tourists around and giving them his undivided attention. No one could deny his knowledge of the history of the Ripper murders. But, the spectators were getting value for money on this particular night.

Ann pursued every lead with keen determination and questioned Richard several times about his conclusions on each case. Richard would cast her a sideways glance with a slight flinch of irritation as he continued to talk to the other non-questioning observers. This would not deter Ann. She was compelled to question more about the murders in 1888. Not satisfied with the carefully manufactured answers given to tourists, Ann held on to her vision and feelings about these tragic incidents.

She turned around to face us and said, 'You know, the first murder was just a trial run. There were no organs removed ... not typical of the other murders.'

Then she looked off into the distance.

'And I have a feeling there were two or three involved in the murders. One would keep watch. It's just that there were different results each time . . . no consistency.'

The first murder that Ann talked about was not the Martha Tabram killing. It was to be some twelve months later back in Australia that Ann picked up another soul who wanted to be heard. I will explain that discovery later in the story.

The guided tour continued and as we wandered through a rather desolate part of town, Ann said she could smell coffee. She asked Richard if there was a coffeehouse nearby. He said there wasn't, but confirmed that the building two doors down used to be a coffeehouse. Ann continued to use all her senses in a seemingly effortless manner when picking up details around her.

Shortly after, we were feeling a lot more light-hearted as we walked along a well-lit main street. When we crossed over to the other side of the road, I noticed a building with a memorial plaque. It was dedicated to merchant seamen who had lost their lives at sea. This seemed important to me considering my earlier meditation when the word 'sea-scribe' had found its way into my mind. I thought to myself of all the stories these men could tell. What secrets lie shrouded in so many watery graves? This intrigued me and I felt sure that it would have some relevance on the trip.

Meanwhile, Richard was pointing out St Christopher's Church on our left. He said it had been previously known as St Botolph's. His powerful voice echoed down the street and we all listened with interest as we walked.

'The prostitutes of last century would walk around the front of the church, smoking their clay pipes, always keeping a careful eye on any men passing by who may be interested.' His voice was tinged with dry humour when he said, 'They would then go around the back of the church with their clients.'

The tourists clearly enjoyed this story, and as he spoke I was imagining myself being a prostitute in those days. I began to wonder whether I would have felt any fear. Just then, I heard Ann and another woman from our group, Karen, laughing behind me.

I turned around and Ann, still smiling broadly, said to me, 'Were you picking up anything from that church Jeanette?'

I told her what I had just been thinking about, or at least it came so fast to me I thought it was my imagination. This is an example of confusing logic with intuition. Sometimes, we can think things and put them down to straight thoughts or

16

imagination. But as I discovered, we might be intuitively picking something up from our past.

'I hope you don't mind me saying this, but I saw you as clear as day grabbing the back of your skirt, pulling it through your legs and up to your waist at the front.'

Ann explained that the reason for this was twofold. She felt that at that time no knickers were worn, but it also stopped the mud from splashing up onto the skirt.

'You were running from the back of the church to start parading your wares at the front! You were a prostitute!'

Ann found this highly amusing. Well, we all hope to be told something mysteriously intriguing about our past lives, but I certainly didn't expect to be told that little gem!

We continued our tour of the streets of White-chapel, and when we were on our way to the scene of the second-last murder Richard said to Ann, 'Get up here Ann. I want to talk to you.'

Richard was now seriously interested in Ann's knowledge and how she was able to access the information. Ann was uncertain how he would react to the fact that she was a psychic and had a genuine interest in uncovering the more hidden aspects of these crimes. But, she shared her story with him and they had a friendly conversation.

Later, Ann was able to give him some personal material that he found interesting.

At the end of the night Richard gathered us all together in a circle. He began evaluating the crimes and gave the names of three main suspects. Finally, he concluded that M. J. Druitt was the most obvious suspect in the Jack-the-Ripper murders. Ann had a problem with this final conclusion, because it effectively suggested the murders ended in 1888. Ann was sure that the later murders in 1889 were attributed to the same group, despite the fact that they were done differently.

'Wasn't Prince Albert one of the suspects?' Ann had to ask this final question, because she had been picking up the Royal family connection.

'Yes, it has been suggested, but there's no proof around that story.'

By now, Richard was aware that Ann would not let go of any leads she had. Earlier, he had told Ann that he didn't follow psychic phenomena, but he wasn't closed to it either.

Ann's concern was not only for the women who were murdered, but also for the unfortunate and tortured souls who were compelled to carry out such horrific crimes. To use Ann's words, 'Their souls need to be put to rest.'

Our first night in London was coming to an end, and we were all weary from our long flight.

A door to the past had been opened and the first night was only a taste of what was to come on the rest of our journey.

4

The Trinity Mystery

13 October 1998

Today was officially day one of our tour. The thirteen people in our group joined another sixteen people from Canada and the United States on the coach. Ann was concerned about this because she wanted our group to share any psychic insights that we picked up along the way. She was sensitive to the fact that other people might feel uncomfortable around such a 'strange' group of travellers. Nevertheless, there was little anyone could do about the situation. On the way to Trinity College, Oxford, we shared our insights within our own group.

When we arrived in Oxford the narrow streets were crammed with students on bicycles and locals who were going about their everyday activities. We were fortunate that the grounds of the college were open for us to view, as this meant we could visit the ancient church.

As I stepped through the doorway to Trinity Church, a heavy feeling of fear and cold rejection ran through my body. There was almost a physical block when entering the church. Murmurs of uncertainty came from the rest of the group.

We turned to our left and walked up the centre aisle. Ann could sense a man around her who was either a doctor or a lawyer. He was a man of considerable power. At that point, Abi asked us to stand beside her. She was feeling dizzy and nauseous. We all walked towards her and there was definitely a strong energy there.

When Ann spoke it was with complete surprise, 'Oh God! I feel ill. My whole body's going.' Ann began to pick up strongly. 'A man. An older man, either a teacher or a tutor. A young man has to go to the Americas. But this man is so strict. He's telling the young student that he must go for his family's sake.'

Just then I was keen to tell Ann my feelings when I walked up to the front of the church and saw the carving of Venus and the scallop shell. I gave Ann my thoughts about sexuality.

With a furrowed brow she said, 'The teacher or

tutor may have been homosexual. But, I'm getting the strong sense that these young men were expected to live a life of celibacy. And this young one didn't want that life.' She broke off for a moment then asked, 'Is there a place called Coventry?'

Ann knew very little about the UK so when she picked up something it was mostly intuitive. Neither did she have an itinerary, so we explained to Ann that it was an English city that was severely bombed during the Second World War. We also told her that to be 'sent to Coventry' meant you were being ostracised and associated with this is a sense of shame.

It appeared that Ann was picking up on the young man's feelings back then. Chris then said she sensed a young man leaning over and being sick. Ann felt that this man had been abused in some way.

'But, where the others were able to take it ... he was not. He was too sensitive. And I don't think he could keep up with the grades either. He wasn't academically inclined ... somebody holding the purse strings ... I'm getting somebody else is in control of the purse strings?'

'This feels the most unholy place,' Eileen, the eldest member of our group, said. An English woman with a great sense of humour, she was being very serious at this point. 'It's getting so cold in here,' she said.

'I still see this tutor,' Ann said. She was very focused now. 'He's strutting. There's a cane ... but the fear this young student has is that he's not academic. I'm getting another young man. He's a brilliant academic. He may have even helped the sensitive one ... tried to protect him ... help him with his marks.'

Ann asked if anyone could pick up a name. Several people suggested various names and Ann suggested the more we dig, the more we uncover.

'This could be a whole class we're picking up on. I've just seen a beautiful red rosebud. Would people come from Ireland to England to study some new school of learning?'

We discussed this possibility and Ann went on to say that the two boys connected as one.

'I feel as though the sensitive one who couldn't make the grades may have been expelled ... put to shame. He may have even taken his own life. Something has to manifest from all of this on the rest of the trip. I'm still getting the Irish connection. The friend, the academic one who went to the Americas. And I feel his family is very wealthy. I'm getting the likes of the Kennedys or the Churchills. But, we'll leave it and see where it takes us. It'll all fit in somehow.'

Chris then said, 'I just heard "thank you".'

'I firmly believe you did,' Ann replied.

The contrasting themes we experienced centred around cruelty and sensitivity. Power and wealth against the face of fragile youth and innocence, we would find, were to shape the rest of our discoveries.

We walked back to the coach and I began to wonder how this could be connected with Jack the Ripper. Ann explained that time is irrelevant when dealing with spirit. 'We just have to wait and see where spirit leads us.'

She pointed out that when souls pass over they might not be able to move on until they are freed from their earthly existence. 'There are souls who need to be released,' she said.

This was to be a journey of learning new concepts.

With this latest insight we travelled to our next destination, Bladon, the burial place of Sir Winston Churchill and his family. We walked through the little graveyard and saw the humble and intimate resting place of one of Great Britain's most powerful families. At the time of our visit we were unaware of the connection between Sir Randolph Churchill and the Jack-the-Ripper case. Later events led us to some important channelled information about the involvement of Sir

Randolph with the Freemasons, and the link between the Churchill family and Trinity College, Oxford.

Whilst it is widely accepted by many researchers that the Freemasons were involved in the Jack-the-Ripper murders, we gleaned some different insights into this long-held mystery through psychic discoveries. But, at least for now, we were satisfied with the serene environment at Bladon. We headed for the small church beside the cemetery, and this time when I walked in I was compelled to bless myself. I looked for the font that is normally found at the entrance, but could not see one. I walked further into the church feeling a sense of holiness and respect about the place. At least, that's what I thought I felt. Yet, why did I feel a need to bless myself (or protect myself) in this church and not in Trinity Church? Eileen said that she felt the family tradition and sense of unity within the walls of Bladon Church. It was cold admittedly, but it was very different from the atmosphere at Trinity, which Eileen was still finding difficult to forget.

Ann, however, felt it was a desolate place and that being buried there meant that the past would remain silent and secluded.

5

Shakespeare's Secrets

13 October 1998

How I had longed for the next part of our tour. We travelled to Stratford-upon-Avon to see the birthplace of William Shakespeare. We walked towards Shakespeare's home and I couldn't help feeling that I was in a modern town which had been stripped of all its former character. The home itself looked 'quaint' and had certainly been well renovated. The gardens were still partially in bloom even though it was mid-October. But along with the carefully manicured gardens and polished floors, there was a sense that the real character of the home had been lost in the renovations.

On our way into the house a middle-aged man stopped and asked me if I would like him to take a photograph of our group. I saw this as a good opportunity and handed my camera over to the stranger with a couple of simple instructions. The picture never turned out. There was something about this home that didn't feel right with me. As soon as we entered the house I felt nothing on the ground floor. It had no atmosphere. And whilst the guides were cheerful in telling the history of Shakespeare's home, it felt very much like a commercial venture which provided little in return for those who were captured by the great writer's past. From a spiritual point of view, I felt utterly disappointed.

Just as I was nurturing this frustration we were invited to go upstairs. When I reached the top of the stairs I felt very dizzy. Now, there was definitely a lot of energy here. And why was it so different from downstairs? The tour guide answered that question. We were standing in the original part of the home. The fireplace at the top of the stairs was the oldest part of the building. We all gathered around the window across from the fireplace. It was here that Ann and the others began getting information. As Ann looked out onto the courtyard she saw a different picture to the modern-day pedestrian walkway.

'There's a woman with red hair looking out of

this window. She's anxious. I can hear horses coming along the cobble-stoned road.'

Chris said, 'Pregnant?'

Ann instantly replied, 'Yes. And the woman has a connection with the sea ... ships, captains. I think she miscarried. She's waiting for the doctor. There's an awful feeling of spotting.'

Chris continued to work with Ann tapping into more details about the woman.

Ann continued, 'She's turning something over and over in her hand. It's round ... gold ... on a chain.'

As Ann spoke her fingers were making the movement of turning an object over. She had the now familiar gaze of concentration on her face as she picked up more information about this mysterious woman. Meanwhile, the wind was howling through the window. Later, when I listened to my tape recording, the sound of the wind evoked an atmosphere that was cold and troublesome.

Ann suddenly said, 'This wasn't the first time. I see her holding on to the end of a bed while someone's tightening a whalebone corset. They're pulling too tight.'

By this time the sound of the wind was terrible and I struggled to hear Ann's words when I played back the tape. But I did manage to hear the rest of it.

'She fainted.'

Ann was now keen to get more information to find out whether what she was picking up could be confirmed. The English tour guide upstairs gave Ann as much information as possible and established that there were miscarriages in the family. He went on to explain that Shakespeare's father was a commercial trader and he had hoped that William, being the eldest of the sons, would eventually take over the business.

'William was fifty-two when he died, but the other brothers all died in their late thirties.' The tour guide answered Ann's questions with a look of curiosity.

'Were they gay?' Ann asked.

'Oh, young men in those days didn't marry until they were in their late twenties, although none of William's brothers did. They didn't have any children. So, you see there was nothing unusual in that. One of the three boys remains a mystery. No one really knows about him.'

By this time the guide was beginning to realise that Ann's questions were along a different line to those of other tourists. She asked if Shakespeare had any female relatives with red hair. The tour guide could not confirm this because there were no portraits of her. Even the portraits of Shakespeare were considered questionable. His interest in Ann reflected Richard's interest in London whilst on the Jack-the-Ripper tour.

'I have to ask you,' he said, 'where are you ladies from?'

Ann explained where we had come from and the purpose of our journey. He was certainly intrigued.

The tour guide began to chat informally to us and our group's laughter brought some warmth to the old home. This is despite the fact that Ann picked up many arguments between William Shakespeare and his wife in the adjacent bedroom. About six months after I returned to Australia I came upon some significant facts about the great writer. Shakespeare was extremely wealthy. (The tour guide mentioned that in today's figures he would have to be earning at least six hundred thousand pounds a year.) I read that in his will he left his many properties to the male heirs of his daughter, Susanna. Sadly, she only had one daughter who survived. And to his wife, he bequeathed his 'second-best bed'. When I thought about what Ann had said on the tape about their arguments in the bedroom, this seemed ironic.

Later, we were directed to the back of the house where we could look down on the back-yard. Ann asked if the wrought iron gates were new as she was getting wooden gates, and she was picking up something about dead animals. She actually said to me that she thought that there were some pets buried in the backyard. Once again, we were enlightened. It used to be a factory yard and there was a tannery out there many years ago!

Whilst all of this was going on I was recording what I had been picking up. I kept getting 'tall poppy syndrome'. I just felt that someone had a high opinion of himself or herself and they had been cut down to size. This was accompanied by a feeling of dizziness. I asked the tour guide to help me out with what I'd been getting. He said that Shakespeare was well respected but that his father was an arrogant man who got himself into a lot of financial trouble with his commercial trading business. He definitely had enemies. Most of the information we channelled that day was confirmed. Ann felt strongly that the tannery had something to do with the intrigue of Victorian times and Jack the Ripper. Despite the early stages of our tour, these correlations would soon be realised.

On a final note, Shakespeare had no name on his gravestone. It was as though his identity remained hidden. Like the Churchills, he was a powerful and well-known man, yet his resting place belies his position in history.

Much has been said about Shakespeare's sexuality but nothing has ever been confirmed. I have a recording of Ann discussing her feelings about a connection with the theatre and the common practice of cross-gender roles in Shakesperian plays. I must point out here that Ann knew nothing of Shakespeare's history or of the myth behind this legendary man. All of Ann's information was derived from her intuitive source and was confirmed through research on returning to Australia. There were other more personal factors that could not be correlated, but they were no less authentic as far as Ann was concerned. She could never ignore the messages she received.

As a light postscript, Ann said that she felt Shakespeare had the skinniest, knottiest legs!

6

Coventry Cathedral's Cleansing

13 October 1998

Broken glass ... shards of glass. Blood smeared, trying furiously to soak up all this blood. So much blood. Can't shift it, can't soak it all up. Stained glass ... stained clothes. Unable to pay the fees asked ... shame and humiliation. The same shame and humiliation is taken to the grave. The need in the next life to feel the need to pay a debt ... the memory and feeling of shame.

I had written these notes on the way to Coventry. I was uncertain what I was writing about, but I just allowed the pen to flow.

'Man's inhumanity to man,' the tour director quoted, whilst talking about the bombing of Coventry during the Second World War.

My thoughts turned to the problem of the poor not being able to pay their fees. I was trying to record this but my tape recorder kept cutting out. I realised that I was bringing my own opinion into the channelling of information. So instead, I decided to pick one of my angel cards to find out what issue we were dealing with here. I got the angel of 'Sexuality'.

Once again this theme was being pushed by spirit and needed to be addressed. We had just left Shakespeare's home and Ann had questioned the sexual preference of the writer and his brothers. It also made me reflect on St Botolph's Church and the prostitutes who worked the area.

There was no doubt that on this psychic tour we were being directed to follow very strong leads. This was only the first day of the tour, but already a pattern was emerging. It was a jigsaw puzzle of sorts, and the final picture would only be pieced together with time and patience.

7

The Yorkshire Moors

14 October 1998

We were slowly getting to know one another within the group, and I decided to speak to Karen on our way to York. Karen was a widow in her thirties. Her manner was elegant and she was a little reserved. A tall, slim woman, she had an air of refinement about her. Whether it was the way she carried herself or her habit of staring wistfully into space I'm not sure, but there always seemed to be a distance between her and the moment. I broke the ice by doing some basic numerology for her, and pretty soon we were discussing the significance of this simple method of divination.

We were driving through the Yorkshire Moors where the murderess Myra Hindley had buried her young victims back in the 1960s. It is a bleak and windy place, covered in scrub and little else for miles. The families and the people of Britain have never forgotten the fate of those children. I can remember the horror of the black and white news reports, and my mother's shock when hearing that a woman had committed those heinous crimes. Since then we have had the 'Yorkshire Ripper', Peter Sutcliffe, who was a seemingly quiet man but harboured a great deal of anger towards women. The energies of such crimes linger on long after the event.

When I finished writing my notes Ann called me over. She had a tape recorder in her hand and was keen to tell me something. She was investigating the link between Trinity College and Jack the Ripper, and was recording her feelings about the regeneration of a negative energy. She was getting Hitler's name as an example. Ann continued to talk about the prolific body snatching for experimentation that occurred in the 1800s. She kept getting a doctor of the Royal Family who was helping young Prince Albert, also known as Prince Eddy. Ann was becoming engrossed in her detective pursuit and was determined to pick up more details. Her need to dig deeper and unravel every clue is very strong within her character. The whole mystery seemed such an enigma to me, and I wondered how it would ever be put together. I'd certainly never been in the company of someone with Ann's psychic abilities who was so tenacious in her pursuit to uncover the answer to this problem.

Most of us in the group were unable to keep up with Ann's energy. Once she gets motivated there is no stopping her. Less than a year before the trip Ann was recovering from bowel cancer. It amazed me how she managed to continue working in Australia and organise and take part in this tour. Such was her determination to follow this mystery.

'I think there's a book in this you know.'

Ann was serious and looked at me waiting for my response. I agreed with her that events were falling rapidly into place and that something needed to be explored and unveiled.

She said to me, 'What about you writing the book?'

I asked her why she couldn't write it. She flip-pantly replied that she was never any good at spelling and didn't finish her high school education.

'Well, I've only had a couple of things published, but I'm really interested in what's happening here.' So I let Ann know that I was willing to go along with it. After all, I had been scribing since the tour began with the intention of writing something about our trip.

* * *

Our next stop was York. York is a beautiful city. The buildings are grand, awe-inspiring works of architecture. We walked along the narrow streets enjoying the sunshine despite the bitterly cold wind that swept through the old district. Leaning forward into the blustery autumn wind, we pushed on until we found a warm, typically English pub where we could have lunch. We sat together chatting about our ancestry and Chris told us about her past life connections going back to the 1920s. Past lives can be interesting, but a lot of people are sceptical about the thought of having lived before.

All of this helped warm our thoroughly cold bodies. With a hot meal in our bellies we took to the streets of York to find out what was in store. There were quite a few shops that sold tarot cards and mystical gifts and some of us bought little reminders of the old city. As we walked through the streets we saw flyers for the 'Great Ghost Walk'. We filled our time until seven o'clock when the ghost walk began.

It was still very cold that night, but fortunately it was dry. Our host wore a black cape and spoke in a strong, theatrical tone. He had an off-beat sense of humour and his quirky comments about Australians left us in no doubt that this would be a light-hearted evening. Quite a few people strolled into the crowd and there was a geniality amongst them.

However, as the night went on it was clear that the stories told were communicated in such a way that the tourists were not expected to take any of this seriously. It encouraged cynicism. In fact there was an element of mockery about the dead, which didn't sit comfortably with us at all. This feeling culminated when the guide spoke of a little girl who had been trapped in a house during the Great Plague. Tragedy is tragedy, and we could not help but feel for the lost soul of the child who had been trapped. And, there is always the question of what happens to the soul who dies in such dire circumstances. The material body disappears, but the lost soul may be searching for release from its confusion and fear.

Most of the other participants seemed to enjoy the evening as a form of light entertainment. But we were on a psychic tour and had very different feelings about those who had passed on. Nevertheless, it was a reality check for us. We were exposed to other people's views on the mystery of spirit. I pointed out to Ann that it might well reflect how some people would view this book. We both agreed that we had no control over other people's responses and, most importantly, it was not for us to judge or be concerned about the material outcome. All we had to do was tell the story as it unfolded for us with the help of spirit.

8

A Tale of Two Cities

15 October 1998

Before leaving York, Ann stood up at breakfast in our hotel and spoke to the rest of the travellers. She wanted to let the group from Canada and the United States know what we were doing and why. They sat quietly and listened to what she had to say. But it was clear that some of them were more traditional in their beliefs and found it difficult to accept an invitation to join our spiritualist gathering. Ann could do no more than ask them if they would like to participate in our venture. She offered this in goodwill and with a sense of openness and honesty.

Understandably, there were those who didn't want to become involved in our adventure. The Australian crew was to remain somewhat divided from the others on the coach. This is not to say that we didn't get along, because by the end of the tour there was fun, laughter and singing from everyone on our travels through the UK. They joined in with our frivolities and, in doing so, accepted who we were and what we were doing.

On our way to Scotland we stopped off at Hadrian's Wall. We stood beside the Roman wall in the cold sunlight. Ann touched the stone and saw soldiers who had been brought from their overseas lands to this desolate place. She could feel their weariness and desire to be back in their own country.

'They're wondering what they're doing here. They can't understand the need to be here.' She felt their utter exhaustion, and their confusion about constructing a wall of defence that had little to do with their lives and homeland.

The themes of power and sacrifice were felt at this spot where the Roman emperor had made his mark through the efforts of ordinary men. Eileen was finding it hard to contain her emotions at the scene. Others comforted her, but the sadness was undeniable.

* * *

Whilst I was writing this part of the book in Australia Ann started to pick up the hopelessness that these souls still feel. She was getting the words, ' "Why were we brought to this god-forsaken place?" They were forcibly taken to a place that they hated. It was so cold and unforgiving. They were ill equipped to do a soldier's job. And they were beaten for their so-called failures. And the only time they could find peace was to look over the water and visualise home. And this is where the sadness lies. They knew that they would *never* return home to die amongst their loved ones. Their lives ended with the enemy all around them. I'm also getting that some even committed suicide. There was an enormous amount of corruption around them. The officers were living very comfortably, and I feel they may have even embezzled the soldiers' wages.'

With no love and little resources, is it any wonder that these simple men felt utter despair? The souls were simply looking for release.

* * *

As we drove further north a vision appeared on a hill in front of us. It was a magnificent sight. The Angel of the Dawn stands atop a hill on the way into Gateshead. It was the most gentle welcome to any city we had seen so far on our trip.

We were now on our way to my homeland,

Scotland. The weather gradually improved and the scenery changed as the hills came into view. Everyone commented on the beauty of the rugged Scottish countryside. I was getting very excited about visiting one of the most beautiful countries in the world.

Once we checked in to our hotel in Edinburgh, we were all glad to simply relax and write in our journals. That evening we took a double-decker bus into the city, which seemed to amuse some of our Australian contingent. As we walked through the streets of Edinburgh, we noticed that there was a ghost tour being held at half past nine that night. We were very fortunate to happen on so many ghost tours! And we were now familiar with the inexpensive pub meals that were available in the UK. For some reason, I was selected to haggle with the publican for our thirteen meals. I followed orders merely to perpetuate the myth that Scottish people are meant to be shrewd when it comes to money!

It was very chilly by the time we left the pub. We waited to hear the young tour guide give us a brief run down on the evening's walk. The theatrics were still there, but this young man was from Edinburgh and he was an historian. I liked his straightforward approach and his dry sense of humour. Edinburgh is a fascinating city. What makes it fascinating is the fact that there is a city below the city.

The Great Plague of 1664 meant that Edinburgh had to be buried and built again. The Plague seemed to symbolise, like Coventry, the purging of souls for new life to begin. But, what of the souls of those who suffered?

That evening we were escorted through the underground city to see where certain businesses had been hundreds of years ago. It was very intriguing, and we experienced some curious psychic phenomena.

First we walked up a steep, dark side street whilst the young tour guide told us about the history of body snatching back in the 1800s. Ann was interested in who attended the Royal College of Surgeons and in particular, if anyone had been expelled because of unusual practices. Body parts could fetch quite high sums (twenty pounds for a womb) with Burke and Hare being the best known grave robbers in Edinburgh at that time.

Then we entered the underground city of the past. It was dark, damp and cold. We peered around to see where various shops had stood and businesses were conducted. A dim red light cast eerie shadows around us, and I felt rather uncomfortable within the cave-like structure. There was a tendency to hold one's breath and the freezing air further heightened an awareness of spirit around us.

We were standing in an area where there had been a cobbler shop and a tannery. I felt a gentle pull on the leather shoulder strap of my bag. It was faint and I thought that perhaps someone was standing too close to me. However, when I looked around I realised that there was nobody behind me. Ann stood next to me, and without moving her head or body, she asked me to look at her handbag.

'Is my bag swinging back and forth?'

She was holding her leather bag between her legs, and as I looked down I was amazed at the pendulum activity that was going on.

'Yes,' I answered quietly, 'are you moving the bag?'

Ann said that she hadn't moved an inch, but she felt her bag begin to swing furiously. 'It's because we're in the place where they worked with leather. They're curious.'

Ann was perfectly calm about this phenomenon whilst I had to get used to the normality of spirit being around. She insisted that there was no feeling of malice, but a simple interest in our wares! When people are not familiar in dealing with psychic energies it can seem frightening. But, the more we experienced on the trip the more we began to recognise non-threatening energies compared to those of a more malevolent nature.

Once again, we had the association with tanneries. There had to be some significance with the Ripper murders. After the underground tour we all got taxis back to the hotel. We had walked so much that day and night that we were too tired to do any psychic work. Our beds beckoned, and we gladly collapsed into the warmth of them. Tomorrow, we were to be shown around the old city and we had to be refreshed for another full day of information and sightseeing.

9

Chloroform for Women

16 October 1998

When I woke, the sky was dark with heavy clouds and the rain was pouring down. And that's how it would remain for the rest of the day. However, the sight of our host cheered us. We sat on the bus outside the hotel and a broad-shouldered, kilted Scotsman with strawberry-fair hair stepped onto the coach and introduced himself. Billy was going to be our Edinburgh tour director for the day. Everyone loved the sight of this Scotsman in his regalia! His authoritative voice boomed down on us and there weren't many that would put a foot wrong that day. We were transfixed. This was just as well because he had some very important knowledge to impart.

We passed the home of Sir James Young Simpson, a Scottish obstetrician who died in 1870. Billy told us the intriguing tale of how this man discovered chloroform. In 1847, the same year he was appointed one of the Queen's physicians for Scotland, three eminent physicians had visited his home and Dr Simpson asked them to inhale the substance. Simpson's wife returned home to find the doctors lying unconscious.

Simpson had read about the use of ether in surgery, but used chloroform for women in labour. He encountered opposition from both the clergy and other obstetricians. The substance was banned for forty years, but this did not stop him or the Royal Family from using the anaesthetic.

* * *

Whilst researching information on Dr Simpson, I read that his medical writings included material on hermaphroditism. The word Hermaphrodite comes from the two Greek deities Hermes and Aphrodite. Hermes could change his gender, and Aphrodite was known as the goddess of love. In human form a hermaphrodite is someone who has both male and female sexual organs and characteristics. All of this needs to be mentioned because it relates to an early morning phone call I received from Ann when we were back in Australia.

She was picking up the use of an anaesthetic, and a man wearing a dress. However, when she was describing this to me she felt that there was something about the genitals that seemed unusual. She was unable to say exactly what it was, but it was as though the penis was useless. It felt as though 'it was just dangling'. This person could not perform fully as a man and wanted the qualities and attributes of a woman. Ann said that he loved and felt comfortable being in women's clothes.

'They're servant's clothes,' she said. 'His situation is completely hopeless yet he is comfortable with this. He would even wear make up. He's using thick, theatrical make-up!' Ann was channelling this information to me during a Brisbane to Perth phone call, and its significance cannot be ignored.

When Ann picked up on the Ripper murders she felt that Prince Albert, or Eddy as he was known, was more comfortable as a female. Photographs of the day show the Prince in tailored uniforms which highlighted his delicate waistline. He had insisted that his clothes be fitted to accentuate this attribute.

During a channelling session, Ann talked of a man, whom she believed to be the Prince, who would fold his penis down between his legs. This was to allow his partner the enjoyment of caressing a beautiful, soft body like that of a young woman. Ann could feel the sensuous touch of the male partner around the lower abdomen which was soft and without much body hair. This made the Prince feel very loved and nurtured.

'It took away his pain of feeling different. It was the only time he felt comfortable, because he was with those who understood him. But, I also feel that he was fickle in love and would change lovers to get what he wanted. And because of who he was, it was never a problem.'

Sir Arthur Conan Doyle was ridiculed for his Jill-the-Ripper theories, but there is some connection here. Conan Doyle had expressed his view that a man dressed as a midwife could have been the Ripper. We are not suggesting that the Prince was a hermaphrodite or that he alone was the Ripper. It was experimentation with his sexuality and drug-taking that provided the escapism he craved. This made him vulnerable to others who were already involved in the occult.

The Prince would have been unaware of the price that he and the other privileged young men would eventually pay for their transient highs. They never thought of tomorrow or who could be hurt. They lived purely for the pleasure of the moment.

Ann's intuition led her to other information about the grandson of Queen Victoria. She had a strong feeling that he would not carry on the Royal line even though there are stories that he had fathered a child born out of wedlock.

'It's as though he is the weakest of the line ... very impure. And it feels right that his line would never continue.'

* * *

Edinburgh's history continued to enthral us. It was home to many famous people, including Robert Louis Stevenson who wrote *Dr Jekyll and Mr Hyde*. For our purposes, the city contained many clues to the Ripper murders. Sir Arthur Conan Doyle, the famous doctor, spiritualist and author of the Sherlock Holmes novels, came from Scotland's capital. Whilst researching the Ripper murders it was interesting to read that references were made to his detective novels. This puzzling dilemma encouraged some innovative thinking from members of Scotland Yard. It was at this time that new discoveries were being made in medicine and science. Detective work was taking an abstract turn as these new methods were incorporated.

We visited Edinburgh Castle and the mood was light despite the rain and wind that howled across the top of the cliff. I walked behind Karen from the coach to the Castle entry. Then, out of nowhere, a small-framed woman appeared alongside Karen and opened her brolly for her to share. It reminded me of a lady-in-waiting. Karen's elegant appearance almost warranted the attention given to her by this stranger. It felt strongly as though in a past life, Karen had been a woman on her own and accustomed to wealth and sadness. This sensation was highlighted in a much more violent manner when we visited a hotel in the heart of the Scottish countryside. That incident occurred the following day in Strathpeffer on the next part of our journey.

Ann and I stood at the doorway of one of the buildings in the Castle grounds as the sky opened up once again. She revealed to me her beliefs about the Prince.

'What I've been getting is that he was definitely drawn into a life that he ultimately had no control over. And the lies that were told to cover up his sexuality and drug taking just created more of a mess for the Royal Family. His involvement with the Freemasons I feel included some other young men who wanted to push the power barriers even further.'

She stared across the quadrangle and said that the only thing left to do was to fill in the details of the picture. 'We need factual evidence and dates.'

As I listened to Ann, I began to feel excited about the prospect of writing a book. Yet, neither of us knew just how much was to be revealed. More unfolded not only during the trip, but also when we returned to Australia where more detail was to be channelled and more research was acquired.

* * *

Following the visit to the Castle, we all decided to split up and do our own sightseeing of the Scottish capital. I joined Chris and Abi, and we began scouring the bookshops. I needed to find a biography on Sir Arthur Conan Doyle. This need stemmed from an experience back in Australia where a medium had gone into trance whilst in my home.

A few days before the trip began, two psychics visited my home in Perth. We had a meditation in the lounge then decided to go into a room where I gave tarot readings. It was our intention to provide one another with guidance and information from spirit by using tarot cards. Glenice began by asking me to choose five tarot cards. I did this, but just as she began talking something happened that I had never before experienced.

She lowered her head, and her speech changed slightly. She spoke more slowly, and the tone in her voice was a little deeper than normal. Glenice had slipped into trance.

'My name is Arthur and you are my sister.' Glenice spoke these words, but it was through a spirit called Arthur. It is important to point out that 'sister' is not to be taken in its literal sense, but as a 'sister in spirit'. Through Arthur, Glenice talked of the significance of my imminent trip and what it would mean to me. It would expand my consciousness in a way that I had never experienced. Before I tell you what Glenice said next, it is important for me to explain here that I have always enjoyed writing, but there has always been a fear attached. It has left me paralysed at times, and the fear was of being ridiculed.

Glenice continued. She spoke eloquently and the language was somewhat 'dated'. I had never heard her speak in this manner before, and I knew that Arthur, whoever he was, must have been a well-educated man.

He talked of my past life when I swore on my deathbed that I would never write again. There was a suggestion that I had written something that could not be accepted by others at that time. In my past life, I had taken this personally and felt as though my life's work had been pointless.

'They did not understand what you were trying to say.'

The message was that I had to persevere this lifetime and follow my chosen path. Finally, Arthur's words ended, and I felt the presence of spirit surge through my body. It was a strange, tingling sensation that did not come from within, but felt more like an external phenomenon. It was very powerful. When Glenice came out of trance, the other psychic who was there immediately got water for her. Glenice drank large amounts, and apparently this is a common result of trance activity. The medium acts as a conduit, allowing spirit through to pass on messages for those on the earthly plane. The medium can feel extremely drained of energy and will either drink a lot of water or feel very hungry afterwards.

Once Glenice had recovered, we began discussing what had just happened. Glenice said that during trance she could smell a strong hospital antiseptic. She felt it was wartime, and that it was around the early part of the twentieth century. The other psychic responded immediately.

'It was Arthur Conan Doyle. As you were talking I was seeing a man sitting by the bed of a wounded soldier, and he was scribing.'

In the months that followed, I too could smell

the strong odour from time-to-time and I understood that he (Arthur) was trying to make contact
with me.

* * *

Whilst I was in Edinburgh on the psychic tour I
was hoping to find a book on Conan Doyle. After
all, he was from Edinburgh. I followed my intuition and felt sure that I would find something
about the creator of the famous Sherlock Holmes
novels.

I walked into a bookshop on Princess Street,
and directly in front of me I saw a paperback
book entitled *Conan Doyle*. On the cover there
was a picture of a formidable looking man with
pen in hand looking at the camera through
round, metal-framed glasses. I was further
delighted when I saw that it was on sale for only
two pounds!

So, now there would be more to discover, I felt,
to take us deeper into the mystery of the Ripper
case. I was not aware that Conan Doyle was interested in spiritualism. This and other details were
revealed in the biography. He had attended the
Boer War to help in his medical capacity. This
linked in with the information that came from
the two psychics in Australia. Also, he had cam-
paigned for lifesaving equipment for the navy. The

'sea-scribe' meditation was becoming clearer to me. His theories on the Ripper case may be mocked, but cannot be ignored, for this was his era, and he was involved with many famous people at that time.

We walked into another bookshop and I immediately walked towards a shelf which had a book with Freemason symbols on the cover. The *Great Secret of Freemasonry* discussed religion and freemasonry. This may not seem significant to some people, but what has to be remembered is that we were continually walking into situations and events that were linked. The bookshop incident is another example of how we were led to certain places where the printed word would confirm what we had picked up and add new information on our search for more clues.

That evening we all gathered together in Ann's hotel room and practised with tarot cards. It was fascinating watching and listening to everyone tell a story about how they felt when they saw the archetypal images. Everyone's focus was getting stronger. The deeper we searched for clues, the stronger the opposition became. For when anyone decides to unravel secrets of the past, there can be certain energies working against them. In spirit world there are those who want to move on and be released. But, there are those who refuse to see the imbalance of their earthly existence and will try to negate any attempts at uncovering the truth. Our stop in Strathpeffer would prove that there were those in the spirit world who would prefer that secrets of the past be left untouched.

10

The Hermit's Home— Strathpeffer

17 October 1998

We left Edinburgh and began a journey that would take us to my place of birth, Dundee. Chris was upset because she had left her pen in the hotel in Edinburgh. The pen belonged to her father who was a Grand Master in the Freemasons and it had his name engraved on it.

Ann said, 'You weren't meant to write down the secrets you discovered on this trip.'

Perhaps not, but this would not stop others from writing their experiences. Perseverance was an essential quality on this journey.

When travelling through the 'Kingdom of Fife' we had to cross the Forth Road Bridge. Fife is still known as a kingdom because of its strong historical link to the Scottish Monarchy. I was a little nervous about this crossing for one specific reason. A clairvoyant friend of mine in Australia told me during a reading before I left to 'Beware of the Firth of Forth'. She had no idea what or where the Firth of Forth was and had no idea why she was telling me to beware! Nevertheless, we crossed the Firth of Forth and there were no dramas. Fine, I thought, it must have some other connection.

Later that day, just before we reached the Tay Road Bridge which took us to Dundee, the tour director expressed some concern. He said that he wasn't sure if we would be able to cross the bridge because of the high winds. He went on to say that we were lucky to get across the Firth of Forth earlier in the day as they had just closed the bridge because it was swinging and too dangerous to carry traffic! There was the answer. A confirmation that spirit is out there giving us clues to prove their existence. Sometimes the messages seem insignificant, but they are essential if we are to open our sixth sense and be aware that spirit exists.

When we arrived at the old golf town of St Andrews, the tour director suggested that we stretch our legs for a short while. As we stepped off the coach into the icy wind it was hard to decide whether the air was invigorating or simply uncomfortable. Most people were definite that it was 'uncomfortable' and opted for the warmth and shelter of a coffee shop near the water.

I, however, was determined to fight the blustery weather. I climbed on to the slippery rocks engraved with lovers' names, and my body wavered as I tried to stand upright and face the roaring waves. It felt so good to be home. This journey was more than just a physical journey. I didn't understand the meaning behind it all, but there was a powerful, inexplicable force at work. Fate's hand had brought us together for a very important purpose.

The elements pushed the presence of spirit and, even though my hands were frozen, I began writing notes. The child within me felt exhilarated, and the excitement of the Scottish leg of the trip was hard to harness. In Celtic country there's a haunting atmosphere. The mountains, grey skies and howling winds beckon a soul to search for its origins. Soon we would be in a small village nestled among trees, high in the mountains. Strathpeffer was like a hermit's home with its remoteness and quiet surroundings. We were, nevertheless, to discover a rather uncomfortable energy there. Whilst Strathpeffer is a beautiful place, the incidents that took place within the hotel gave us the strong sense that rituals or secret practices had been performed in the region.

We checked in to the hotel and were directed to our rooms. I had no real reason to explain it but I felt scared and unhappy about going into my room on my own. Once I had settled down I began to perform some reiki on myself. Reiki is a form of universal healing. The process is meditative and always helps me to relax. In fact, I was so relaxed that I consequently dozed off, but I had a rude awakening when I heard the door handle behind me rattling. The room was small, and my head was next to the door, so there was no mistaking the sound of someone trying to force the door open. I called out, 'Yes, who is it?' There was no response. I stood up and opened the door. My bedroom was at the end of the hall. I looked down the hallway, but there was no sign of anyone there.

Meanwhile, an alarm kept going off somewhere in the hotel. This actually happened several times. I was glad when it was time to join the others for dinner. Before going into the dining room I asked the receptionist if any of the staff had been trying to gain access to my room. 'Not at this time of night,' was her reply.

At dinner I found out that two women in our group, Ann and Julie, who were mother and daughter, had to be moved from their room because the alarm was being set off for no apparent reason. Both these women were very psychic, and it would seem that their energy was causing problems with the electrical system! We discussed this at dinner, and Julie's mother was perplexed by the problems they had. It had been a very long day, and after drinking one glass of white wine I was ready for bed. That night my sleep was to include visions of many strange symbols and messages.

11

Dreamspeak

18 October 1998

Just before opening my eyes this morning I saw a variety of symbols. Somehow I knew that they were connected to freemasonry and Jack the Ripper. The frustrating part was that I couldn't translate the meaning of the symbols. Then, just at the end, I was shown a circle within a circle. I sat up and drew the shape that I'd seen and began recording the dream I'd had just before the symbols appeared.

In my dream Colleen McCullough was talking to me about being a writer. I knew instinctively, however, that this was to do with Norfolk Island where Colleen McCullough lives and writes. We were looking for a secluded place where there is peace and tranquillity. I felt it had something to do with Prince Eddy. Was he sent to an island for periods of isolation? What was the real truth? It was murky, but there was something hidden that needed to be revealed. The current British Prime Minister, Tony Blair, was also in the dream. He talked of controversial findings within the Royal Family and the Jack-the-Ripper case.

Something was made clearer later in the day. We went to Blair Castle, which seemed to be the link with Tony Blair. But the word 'Blair' means open space, or wide open. There were to be no secrets. A door would be opened and the truth would be exposed. And somehow there had to be a connection with Norfolk.

* * *

We were to visit Loch Ness and the Isle of Skye today. The drive through the Grampians was stunning, and everyone enjoyed the scenery as mountains loomed ahead, some snow-tipped with the first taste of winter chasing the autumn bow. The sky was a brilliant blue and the pine trees stretched across the heart of the rich, brown earth. We passed a large, tranquil loch and a full rainbow appeared to complete the colourful picture. Our tour director talked of the pot of gold we would surely find.

The driver pulled into a lay by, and we could

see that there was some interest by the loch. It was a piper playing a beautiful Scottish lament. He was dressed in vivid blue Scottish attire. His physique was lean for a man in his wisdom years, and he had a sandy coloured handlebar moustache. It was young Julie's birthday that day, and the piper played 'Happy Birthday' for her. We all watched as he gave her his full attention. Julie's mother was delighted, and we were truly thrilled at his warm hospitality. Everyone applauded. It was a very special moment. It was a gift.

As we drove through the more remote parts of Scotland, the tour director began telling us a rather eerie story about a village we were passing. Loch Cluanie had flooded and the villagers had to flee their homes. This meant that many possessions and treasured memories were lost beneath a watery grave. The church, a sanctuary of births, deaths and marriages, was swallowed whole by nature. He continued to describe the uncanny scene in the summer of 1984 when during a drought, the old church began to show through the loch as the water dried up to reveal the mysterious, silent past.

As he talked, I saw scars in the landscape that reflected those lives. They were etched into the mountains, like a vision of sorrow. I watched the sweeping rain, a reminder of the pain and anger of those who had to leave. Repeatedly, I felt the sadness of those who had lost all to the elements. Nature's beauty and harshness could be seen holding hands in this isolated part of Scotland. The curved moss rocks in the knuckled hills were like breasts that protected that sacred home. Its spirit remained forever in that place. It could never be lost. No amount of ravaging could wash away the soul of Loch Cluanie.

Yet again, I was reminded of the 'sea-scribe'. So many secrets buried beneath the rush of water. So many souls ached to be put to rest. This recurring theme nagged deep within my subconscious.

* * *

Two years later, almost to the day, Ann visited me in Perth.

I was living 100 metres from the Indian Ocean, and I was fearful of ever having to leave that place. Amazingly, Ann picked up on my need to be close to the ocean. She was just about to doze off when she yelled out to me to write something down. I did as she said and wrote down her message.

The sea is important to you (me) because you were buried at sea ... the sea scrolls ... I'm actually seeing grey marble, but it's damp with the constant rain

68

battering at the surface ... it's icy cold ... it's been there for centuries ... and nobody has recognised these souls ... but it's not real? It's an image to convey the agony of those who were forgotten, or worse still, who were blamed and left for dead on sinking ships. There are no names? Some even had their identities stolen by others who wanted to erase their past ... not necessarily to do with criminal activities, but to begin new lives and get the respect from others who would treat them like heroes. It's almost as though you're being brought back to the sea to find the answers. It's important for you to let the sea bring up to the surface what you need to know for your future ... it's been buried long enough, and there's a need to bring it out with pride ... you seek to find it where the treasures are locked ... you've got to wait for them to be unlocked. Don't worry, that's why you're so attached to the water.

* * *

The Sea is my Soul

Beneath the ocean, a whale cries
The fish of night swim dark and long
Their destination, known to them.
Where does my lost soul belong?

I push towards my watery past
I pass the lovers' rock,
Initials scarred hard
In sea-washed stone.

The above is a portion of a poem I wrote only a few months before our trip. I had been 'playing' with the idea of writing a book, and the book was called, 'The Sea is my Soul'. This only reinforces Ann's earlier advice, which was to take note of anything that's significant to you, for whatever reason.

Later that night, Ann began to channel the injustices felt by those buried at sea.

'Heroes treated like criminals . . . look at today to see what happened yesterday?'

I interrupted, 'The Greek ferry tragedy!'

Ann nodded. 'Exactly!'

There were those who caused problems, but there were also souls who were never recognised for the valiant role they played in trying to save their vessel and the lives of those on board. This began to open up something deep within me that needed to be expressed.

Ann was still channelling when she said to me, 'When this book's published you'll have the key to the truth about the sea. It will open the chest beneath the sea that will set, not only you, but the other truths free.'

Ann's eyes then began to fill with tears. Her fingers were interlocked, and she looked as though she was in prayer.

She then put her hand on my shoulder and said, 'I'm with you Jeanette . . . I'm with you Jeanette.' Her voice was soft, almost fragile, but it had a determination about it. 'I can't help feeling that it's your mother? She always loved you, but you couldn't see it because she didn't know how to express it. But she sure as hell does now. She's saying to go ahead with the book, and the truth will set you free.'

Those words, 'the truth will set you free', were of great significance. Two days before the trip, I visited St John's Cathedral in Brisbane. I took a photograph of a banner which said, 'The Truth Will Make You Free'. I had that photograph taped to the edge of my computer the whole time we were writing this book. It was an instinctive gesture, which I barely understood at the time.

* * *

The next part of our trip would highlight how some so-called 'heroes' were in fact cowards when it mattered most. We were on our way to the cottage where Bonnie Prince Charlie had hidden. When we walked into the cottage the light was poor and the air constricting. Ann began to pick up on the young Prince saying that he was a coward. He didn't have the confidence without the support of his protectors. Ann could smell fear within the cottage and wasn't particularly comfortable with the feelings she was getting. It's important to note that Ann was not familiar with Scottish history, and what she was picking up was purely intuitive.

Culloden Moor is a desolate piece of land covered in swampy scrub and thistles. A battle took place there in 1746 between the Scottish and the English, and Bonnie Prince Charlie was defeated.

It would be on the last day of writing this book that Ann picked up the sound of bagpipes, and began humming the tune she heard. She asked me what the tune was. 'Scotland the Brave,' I replied. She was keen to talk about William Wallace. By looking at a sketch of this man, Ann felt that he was 'destined' to follow his path of martyrdom. By this she meant that he knew he had a calling to do something, and it wasn't until he became a leader that his destiny began to unfold. He was seen as the mystic and the visionary who could save the poor and the oppressed.

It was his ability to tap into his intuition that helped him in battle. The passionate fire that burned fearlessly within him was the unquestionable loyalty he had for his supporters. This helped him to face every challenge without fear.

However, Ann felt that in the beginning the men who were with Wallace were only there because their masters had ordered them to follow him. But Wallace wanted to see the faces of the nobles and all those in power at his side in battle, and not just their servants. Nevertheless, despite the early ambivalence of his supporters, Wallace eventually won their hearts and their loyalty. And he in turn felt strongly protective towards these men.

Ultimately though, Ann sensed that some of the clans were turncoats. They became fearful of his growing power and status, because the legend of William Wallace filled the hearts of many people with terror. In truth, the legend was becoming greater than the man himself. The way in which he was tortured and murdered showed the amount of fear that others had of him. But, like Joan of Arc, his horrific death immortalised his soul, and ultimately he brought Scotland together.

Following the legend of William Wallace, came the legend of his sword. It is encased within a glass cabinet in the Wallace Monument in Stirling, Scotland. At sixty-six inches in length, and made from heavy Scottish steel, it is said that Wallace would have to be at least six feet, seven inches tall to be able to wield the sword. Ann's feelings on this were that he was between five feet eight and five feet ten. He would have been well built, but not fat.

The strongest feeling Ann had was that his sword was destroyed when he was taken prisoner. His sword was the truth in battle, and it had to be smashed so that it no longer held any mysterious power. But more than that, she felt that his sword was not only smashed but also melted down so that nothing would remain of this powerful symbol. Later, the same power of fire and passion that William Wallace had once instilled in his countrymen would return when the symbol of his sword was again resurrected.

* * *

I had been compelled to watch a few versions of Joan of Arc over the two years that lapsed since our tour. She had mysteriously found a sword to use in battle against the English. This was to be her sword of truth and courage. This young French woman was literally devoted to God. As a child she found utter joy in His union. She wanted to be closer to Him. It would be the threat of English rule over France that would lead her to passionately fight for her country and her God. The visions she experienced led her to be burned at the stake, because the church considered her to be a witch. This young child, who selflessly loved God, was condemned as a witch. Once again we hear of a martyr who was revered by many followers. She was only human. But she was driven. And like William Wallace and King Arthur, she would die and be resurrected as a legend to be honoured. As a final note, it was the women in her family who passed on the nobility of her name.

* * *

The next stop, the Isle of Skye, was even colder than our previous haunt! The isolated island didn't exactly welcome the stranger to its shores, but rather dared one to stand awhile in the Nordic-style land and consider the possibility of getting back on the bus. Nevertheless, we hoarded into the local restaurant, had some piping hot soup and chatted whilst keeping ourselves warm.

Ann talked of the sacrifices she had made to ensure that this trip went ahead. Until now, I hadn't realised just how much this tour meant to her. She had a single-pointed vision and was in no doubt about the importance of the Jack-the-Ripper case.

By the time we got back to our hotel in Strathpeffer and had dinner we were ready to do some channelling. As we sat in the lounge area of the old hotel I couldn't help noticing the sign over the archway to the dining room. It was a commemorative plaque of the Victorian era. The year was 1888. All very timely.

Ann began by picking up on a few people in our group. She looked at Julie and said, 'You're someone who knows secrets, and knows how to keep them. It's as though you are privy to a lot of information, but can't tell anyone what you know. It's your position. And you're really anxious because you need to keep this wall of silence.'

Ann then began getting the feeling that Julie was a carriage driver. She was male, and there was a great urgency to get a baby into the carriage and take off. Ann felt that the person who had been entrusted with the infant was either a bishop or an archbishop.

'This man wore a large, gold ring with a red stone.'

Julie's mother then said that she also picked up on the ring and felt it was a garnet.

Ann continued talking to Julie. 'But, you

thought the carriage would be inconspicuous. I'm getting a feeling that you've just spotted something that would be a give-away. You're holding the reins, and you see the horse on the right side. As it turns its head you can see the Royal Crest is showing on the blinkers. You hadn't thought of that!'

Our later research found that there was a Royal Coachman called John Netley. He appears to be the person Ann was picking up when she was channelling one of the Ripper murders.

Meanwhile, Julie said that she had always felt an anxiety for others. 'It's like I'm responsible for them,' she said. 'And horses are my love. I was brought up on a farm and they're the way I relax.'

The story about the baby being rushed away in secrecy was a mystery to us at this point.

Julie, as I mentioned earlier, was very psychic. However, this session touched a nerve deep within her. She felt a little uneasy about the suggestion that she was the coach driver. There was a fear of exposure, which manifested as a flippant attitude towards Ann's channelling. But Ann stayed with it, because she knew that what she said to Julie would eventually make some sense. Somehow, it was the key to an unsolved mystery in her present life. She left it at that.

Ann then turned to Julie's mother whose name is also Ann.

'I'm getting someone who is a Lady and she plays bridge. You look after the family estate when your husband's away. There seems to be a French connection. I'm getting scars on your scalp and neck?'

Julie's mother told Ann that she did indeed have scars on her scalp. Angie and Christine were two of the younger women on the trip and Ann felt that they were two royal children.

Chris from Tasmania was very intuitive and she had worked with Ann when we were in Shakespeare's home. Ann felt that Chris had been a man who had gambled constantly and lost a lot of money on deals.

'You won a home in a bet. But, it didn't have any furniture in it. And you weren't able to sell it for some reason. You were really furious about it because it meant you couldn't keep gambling.'

Ann felt that the house was near water. It's interesting to know that Chris works in a gambling institution and lives in a home by the beach. This amused Chris, but even more so when Ann told her that as a man she had also been interested in other men!

Finally, Ann was getting a strong feeling about

Karen. Karen was the young widow I mentioned earlier.

'Your mother keeps trying to marry you off. But you don't want that. You're very elegant, and there's a sadness there but you really can't be bothered with marriage.'

This last incident was of importance. Princess May of Teck's mother had always been looking for a suitable partner for her daughter. Queen Victoria has been recorded as saying that Princess May was too royal to marry a commoner, but not royal enough to marry into the Royal Family. Yet, as history shows us, she would be the only woman willing to take on the challenge of marrying Prince Eddy in order to save her family.

Karen listened to Ann and then told us of her experience whilst having a bath in her hotel room. She had a strong feeling that someone was spying on her. It terrified her so much that she had to get out of the bath and get dressed. Then, she was about to go to sleep when something shocked her.

'I was just lying there when I felt someone kick the end of the bed. And they were angry! I physically felt the kick, and I was scared!'

Julie's mother began talking about the restless night they had too.

'I watched Julie all night. She was tossing and turning and talking in her sleep. I was almost too frightened to go to sleep in case something happened to her.'

At this point I hadn't told anyone about my experience with the rattling door handle, but now I felt a lot more comfortable about mentioning it.

What really surprised me was that Ann had been frightened in her hotel room too! It was about 1:00am and she was doing a radio connection to South Australia.

'I was on the phone and there was a mirrored wardrobe door behind me. I just had the awful feeling that if I looked around at it I would see something. Because, if spirit wants to show itself, that's one way that it can come through. But, I had this apprehension and deliberately looked the other way while I was on the phone. It was scary.'

* * *

As I've mentioned, Strathpeffer is a very secluded place, so I was surprised to see it mentioned in a book about the life of Queen Mary. James Pope-Hennessy wrote of the Royal Family's home in Sandringham. This is where Prince Eddy was to die in mysterious and tragic circumstances. He described how the original home was burned almost to the ground in 1870, and how the Prince of Wales, Prince Eddy's father, had 'constructed a strange long mansion of harsh orange brick and white stone'. He said that the house resembled 'a station-hotel in Strathpeffer'. The young Prince was only seven years old when his father resurrected the house. Twenty-one years later it would be the place where he would spend his last, agonising days.

The Prince of Wales was a 'Most Worshipful Grand Master of English Freemasons'. The secrecy of freemasonry has been a block for serious investigations into the Ripper murders. Ann was sure that more than one person was involved. Indeed, Prince Eddy was suspected, but his involvement would appear to be only part of a much more powerful and corrupt group. Whilst channelling in Australia, both Ann and I sensed the fragile helplessness of a young Prince who was continually demoralised by his father.

Through his mother's efforts, the Prince was introduced into the artistic and literary society of London. The Princess of Wales had asked the artist Walter Sickert to introduce Eddy to his circle of friends. The Prince's life became out of control. Many outside pressures weighed upon this young man who was earnestly seeking love and approval. It became clear to us that London's literary and artistic circle was aware of the Prince's entanglement, and could only reveal certain details within their creative work. This began to unfold whilst we were in Wales. I had been drawn to an Oscar Wilde book whilst Ann had been hunting down a book on May of Teck. However, we will look deeper into this area later in the book.

I mention the Prince of Wales' connection to the Freemasons because it was in Strathpeffer that I received the images and symbols of freemasonry. Also, the link to Norfolk was established in my dream. Sandringham House is in Norfolk where Prince Eddy died. It seems like an odd collection of details, but the significance was to become clearer as our journey continued.

That evening I had the urge to use my Egyptian cartouche to find out more about Jack the Ripper. In the past position was Uraeus. Uraeus represents the serpent within. It has to do with occult powers and can be described as 'he or she who takes total control'. In the present position was Set, known as the manipulator. Adverse energies abound with Set that can cause obstacles or delays. We were certainly experiencing adverse energies within the hotel. Set is also known as the Prince of Darkness, the enemy of Osiris and Horus. So then, what was in the near future? It was Horus. Horus is the redeemer, and the patron saint of homes and families. He helps the spiritually oppressed to hold firm when difficulties arise. Finally, the distant future card was the Scarab. The Scarab is spiritual renewal. It brings in new energies that clear away the old and heralds a new day.

I sat on my bed and looked at the cards. I had been led to create this spread and the message appeared clear to me. We were now investigating the occult dealings of the past. The current problems we were experiencing would soon be overcome, and a resolution would be found in the future to clear away the deeds of the past and help free these trapped souls. I recorded everything I'd discovered and settled down for the night, albeit a little uncomfortably.

12

'I'm the King of the World!'

19 October 1998

We left Strathpeffer and were able to have some relaxing time on our own. We were given a few sightseeing options, and I decided to go on a cruise across Loch Lomond. Some of the younger members of the group were on the boat, and we had a wonderful day.

We all inhaled great lungs full of fresh Scottish air. As usual, it was icy cold but the sun shone most of the way. There was a lot of laughter on this part of the trip. We were not involved in any search for clues or listening to tour guides. Abi was so enthused that she ran up to the end of the boat, and leaning over cried, 'I'm the king of the world!' Clearly, the atmosphere had evoked this spontaneous rendition from the movie 'Titanic'. However, this innocent outburst turned out to be a direct revelation the next day.

The cruise on Loch Lomond continued and we were shown the cave where Rob Roy Macgregor hid. The boat stopped at the deepest part of the loch and everyone fell silent for a moment. I gazed at the pine trees on the rich, green hillside and the snow-tipped mountains that surrounded us. I thought of the terror that must have filled Rob Roy, and how this beautiful sanctuary was once a place of fear and battle. My thoughts were interrupted as jets of water sprayed from the loch across the front of the boat and we continued our journey through some of the most serene countryside in Scotland.

We finished the cruise and met up with the others on the coach. Our next visit was the Burrell Collection of Fine Art in the city of Glasgow, and as we journeyed towards the art gallery I decided to read my book on Conan Doyle. I was intrigued to read that he had an unquenchable thirst for research. Naturally, this would have been essential for his detailed and well-crafted Sherlock Holmes novels, but he was interested in a variety of subjects. He was a voracious reader and was keen to share his knowledge through both his creative and practical work.

When we arrived at the gallery, we all went our own way and wandered through the building soaking up the many displays of artwork. I heard a group of French tourists talking and was compelled to join them. They had gathered around a painting of ballerinas entitled 'The Rehearsal' by the artist Edgar Degas. A guide was informing the group that Degas extensively researched ballet, particularly the physical qualities of the ballerinas. And from this he knew more about ballet than the ballerinas did. I listened intently. This was the second time in a few hours that I had been made aware of the importance of research and its application in art. There was a sense within me that in the years to come I too would become involved in some sort of research. My intuition felt very strong at this point, and whilst no one told me directly that my future would involve research I knew somehow that it would. I also felt that it would take some years to 'rehearse' my art.

I began to think about art and the artist's desire to create something of beauty. Degas had a desire to express his feelings through his painting of the ballerinas. Their discipline and dedication to their art involved painful endurance, and above all, a love for their chosen expression of art. Later, when

I talked to one of the tourists on the trip, she felt that Degas did not understand the pain suffered by the ballerinas. Mary was an American who was with the other group of travellers on the tour. She told me that she had been a ballerina for many years, and said that Degas never showed the faces of the ballerinas. He clearly showed the features of the Grand Masters, but never the faces of those who endured the physical expression of their art.

I listened to her words, but felt that Degas would also have struggled and suffered in order to express his higher self. I wondered how this could have anything to do with Jack the Ripper, but it is worth pointing out that 'The Rehearsal' was painted somewhere between 1878 and 1879 when Prince Eddy was about eighteen years of age.

Whilst following up some research after the trip I was drawn to briefly examine Prince Eddy's astrological chart. There was a strong possibility that he could have been attracted to spiritual or artistic partners. There seemed to be confusion around his partners and around his sexuality whilst searching and yearning for a higher love. The manner in which he attained that higher love could have been expressed in a variety of ways. If Prince Eddy had become involved in spiritual practices or in the depth of his artistic soul then he may have avoided the other outlet available for heightening his sense of self-love. But the Prince chose a mind-altering state to escape his own vulnerability and the lack of love from his parents. Drugs and alcohol provided the escapism he desperately needed. I firmly believe that he was a tortured soul, despite his excessive behaviour and disruptive lifestyle. Artists suffer whilst trying to express their own inner beauty, but in their expression they are recognising their gifts. Sadly, the young Prince never did this. Degas portrayed both pain and beauty which, I feel, reflected the life and image of Prince Eddy.

13

Excitement at the Adelphi

20 October 1998

We were having breakfast at our Glasgow hotel and discussing the events of the previous day. Abi's playfulness on board the boat at Loch Lomond brought forward the subject of the *Titanic*. Ann told us that during the night she saw herself as a very wealthy woman. She was wearing a coat with a fur collar and it had something to do with the *Titanic*. But this woman had no fear, Ann said. She felt a connection somehow, but had no real reason for this. I was getting the young wife of John Jacob Astor, but like Ann I had no rational explanation for this.

One of the gentlemen from the other group overheard our conversation.

'There's a special section in today's newspaper about the sinking of the *Titanic*.'

We just looked at one another. Another unbelievable link had been presented to us.

The newspaper had a pull-out section about the tragedy, listing names and the sequence of events. I managed to secure a copy of the paper before boarding the coach to Liverpool.

* * *

When I was writing this section of the book, I couldn't let go of what Ann had said and rang her to find out if she could get any more information. She pursued Astor's history and discovered that he was the great grandson of William Waldorf Astor, major fur trader and merchant. Hence, Ann's need to talk about the fur collar. Furthermore, she picked up that Mrs Astor was wearing brown, soft leather shoes with a square tongue.

Whilst researching the story of the *Titanic* disaster we discovered that John Jacob Astor, first cousin of the British politician Lord Astor, was not perturbed about their dire circumstances. In fact, he and his young pregnant wife were in the gymnasium on the mechanical horses whilst everyone else was scrambling to get on the lifeboats. The young eighteen year old obviously trusted her forty-six year old husband's feelings that the surrounding panic was to be ignored. He was adamant that they were safer on the *Titanic* than in a small boat. We now understood why Ann said the woman with the fur collar had 'no fear'.

We felt as though this was all the information that we would get on the Astors. However, a year later when Ann came to Perth to help finish the book she began feeling the presence of a young woman who seemed lost. Ann walked toward the chair next to mine at the computer when she saw her staring wistfully into some place far away.

'She was hurt. Her mother felt that shame had been brought to the family because of the gossip that her young daughter was sleeping with a much older man.'

The young woman Ann saw was Madeleine Astor.

Ann picked up that the young Mrs Astor was not interested in her husband's money, but was more fascinated by the man himself. She was seeing him as a father figure and a protector. Ann felt that she was extremely soft and sensitive. All of this caused us to do some research on Mrs Astor. One report said that she had committed suicide in 1937. Another report simply stated that she died of a heart attack in 1940. The death certificate confirmed that she died on 27 March 1940 at the age of forty-six, which was the same age as her husband when he died. The certificate itself was limited in information, yet it highlighted a very interesting fact. Mrs Astor's permanent address was given as the hospital address where she had been staying 'intermittently'. Ann and I both felt that there was a history of depression. In Miami, Florida, there is no public access to cause of death. Did she commit suicide as had been reported? We did not delve too deeply into the wounds of this woman's life.

Knowing that her wealthy husband's will stated that she would receive his inheritance only if she remained a widow, tells us a lot about John Jacob Astor. In death, as in life, he would never let her go. If she could not be with him, then she could not happily be with anyone else. All the wealth that she could have had, she forfeited. Money was never the issue. Was the wistfulness that Ann saw in this young woman a reflection of her being pulled to be with her husband on the other side?

Perhaps she never lived a 'real' life after the *Titanic*, and was forever held in its memory and loss. The day her husband died Madeleine Astor remained tied to the ghost of this man, as surely as if she had gone down on the *Titanic* with him, and she would never have understood what was pulling her back. It has been stated repeatedly that she did not want to leave him on the ship.

* * *

We drove around George Square in Glasgow and the tour director told us that Queen Victoria had opened the Square in 1888. There was a statue of the Scottish writer Sir Walter Scott. The guide quoted his famous words, 'Oh what a tangled web we weave, when first we practise to deceive.' I wrote this down and thought of Queen Victoria. I stared across at George Square and the statue of the Queen. What secrets did she hold?

Whilst on the bus we were beginning to have a real sense of excitement about all of this.

'I have some excellent news for you all.' Our tour guide told us that on our arrival in Liverpool we would be staying at the Adelphi hotel.

'It's a beautiful hotel,' he said. 'And it's where they actually filmed the ball scenes for the *Titanic* movie.'

Ann and I just stared at one another. No words were exchanged. This was becoming more and more bizarre! Finally, Ann said to me that she felt as though a door was being held open for us on this trip.

'It's only going to be open for a short time. We're getting all the help we need to recognise these souls and their tragedy.'

By the time we reached Liverpool and the grand hotel we were all on a high!

* * *

Arthur Towle acquired and rebuilt the Adelphi in 1912, the same year as the sinking of the *Titanic*. Standing in the foyer of this opulent hotel made us feel excited, almost as though we were part of that decadent era. It had an energy that grabbed you, that made you want to have fun! I looked up at the mirrored ceiling then down at the tiled floor, amazed at the richness of it all. Statues, vases and ornaments of colonial times decorated the grand foyer. It positively screamed its history at you. The imagination did not have to work hard to recapture the earlier days of socialites and entertainment.

As I turned the door handle and entered my room I could feel the exhilaration of years gone by. I had a feeling that I wanted to dance and play music, so I turned on the radio and danced across the room. The only thing missing was a bottle of champagne on ice. The rooms were richly deco-rated and so spacious! That night, we all decided to wear evening dress to dinner.

The atmosphere at dinner was very different to any other hotel on the trip. We were on our best behaviour for one thing! When we finished our meal, we walked through the hotel to investigate the various rooms. Ron had his video camera and he filmed us as we all wandered around admiring the architecture and grand scale of the building.

The chandeliers lit up the enormous rooms, but there was one room that was almost in complete darkness. We walked through the Empire Room and cast our gaze at the enormous, rectangular table, which was surrounded by richly ornate chairs. The chair at the head of the table was obviously for the Grand Master, for this appeared to be the Freemasons' function room. There were Freemason symbols all around the high ceilings and the chairs were also hand carved with the same detail.

No one dared to touch or sit on the imposing throne at the head of the table. The air of power and respect had us on our guard somehow. But Ron had very different ideas. What he did next not only surprised us, but made us fearful. He walked towards the head chair and with a defiant grin, sat on the Grand Master's throne. There was a silence from the rest of us, an awful sensation that his actions would lead to some uncanny fate. It was as though the sword of Damocles hung over his head. This is not an exaggerated account of what happened. The experience was very real. Ron was the only male on our trip, and perhaps there was a sense of male daring in all of this, but we couldn't help feeling uncomfortable about what he'd done.

The following morning Ron did not come downstairs for breakfast. His wife said that he was ill and wouldn't be joining the group that day for the coach tour.

On our way out to the coach we asked about the Empire Room. The receptionist told us that it was used for the Masonic Lodge and that they met on Thursday nights. Ann's whole feeling about the Empire Room was that there had been a lot of 'backstabbing . . . cloak and dagger stuff going on'. In fact, she had a strong sense that younger men were involved who wanted to push the boundaries of freemasonry. This made sense of the 'circle within a circle' that came to me in Strathpeffer. Ann had a feeling that they wanted to revive the experiences of the ancient order and the so-called power that the rituals provided.

'For too long the young ones had lived through the stories only vicariously. Now through their drug-induced states they felt they could reach the heights of power through experimentation. They felt invincible!'

* * *

Six months after this event we were back in Australia and I had visited Ann for a week in Brisbane. It was to be a relaxing holiday, but on the last night of my stay something strange happened. It was quite late in the evening and Ann and I were talking in her kitchen. Suddenly, I had to tell Ann that it felt as though someone was standing behind me. Ann looked at me and said, 'It's a man and I feel his struggle to breathe.'

We had been discussing the people who had been on the *Titanic* when this happened. We decided to sleep on this latest insight and perhaps something would be revealed.

The next morning whilst Ann was driving me to the airport she began picking up information about the *Titanic* again.

'I'm getting you as a young man on the ship dressed in black. You have all these pieces of paper, and you're running back and forward with all these messages.'

She felt that I was someone involved in communications on board the ship. I was surprised to hear Ann talk about me as someone who had worked on the *Titanic*. Yet, she clarified something that had been troubling me before my trip to Brisbane.

I had been waking up in the middle of the night to all sorts of sounds which ranged from blips to high-pitched noises. I wasn't sure if it was morse code or something from outer space! But it was always loud enough to wake me. In fact, I had been getting quite annoyed with the constant interruptions to my sleep, however, I recorded these events in my journal.

* * *

When I got back to Perth I attended a Spiritualist church and was given a message which confirmed Ann's feelings about the *Titanic*. The woman on the platform chose me as her final reading.

'Are you an inspirational writer?' she asked. 'Because I see all these books around you.'

I nodded, curious to hear what she had to say next.

'Well, I have a tall gentleman with me, and he says it's time for you to look back on what you've written and you'll find the answers you need.'

This was the most direct message I had ever received concerning my interest in spiritual writing.

When I got home, I looked back through my most recent journal and there it was. I had recorded waking up from a dream utterly exhausted because I had been running back and forth non-stop!

It dawned on me that the loud signals I heard during the night and the previous dream were strong messages from spirit about the night of the *Titanic* disaster. There was a correlation between what Ann was getting and my dreams. This turned out to be the way we worked together whilst getting information for this book. It may sound strange and difficult to believe, but spirit tries to connect with us in any way they can. And those messages are rarely straightforward. A good understanding of symbolism and a healthy respect for one's intuitive gifts does make the translation a lot easier!

The story does not end there. The day after I arrived back in Perth from Brisbane, I awoke to phones ringing and beeps and blips that nearly drove me mad. It was confirmation that what we had hit on the night before was important to follow through. Later that morning I was browsing through the local bookstore and I came across a large book of questions and answers on the *Titanic*. My natural curiosity made me open the book and read whatever was on the page.

The question on the page was, 'How long did

Jack Phillips and Harold Bride stay in the wireless room?'

There it was. The communications officers who tried desperately to relay final messages to loved ones were once again trying to make contact. Ann and I felt that we needed to recognise this event in some way. The souls who were lost on the *Titanic* still needed to be released. As I wrote all of this in my journal I realised that it was 'May Day'! This whole event would take on a very personal significance eighteen months later.

* * *

Ann was visiting me, and the final touches were being added to the book. I have mentioned her needing to tell me that she was picking up that I was buried at sea, but there was a grey, marble slab with nothing on it. No names were recorded. Perhaps it is timely to reiterate one verse of my poem.

The Sea is my Soul

Beneath the ocean, a whale cries
The fish of night swim dark and long
Their destination, known to them.
Where does my lost soul belong?

One morning when Ann woke up she told me about a dream she had.

'Last night I was dreaming about your last life. I knew you died, and you were a young man. But, I didn't know your name. I wanted to send flowers, but I didn't have a *name* and there was nowhere to send them. There was no record of you! Then the dream moved forward in time. I knew that in this life you were "Han".'

Ann then explained that she had seen a deep green, lush laurel of olive leaves. This, she said, was symbolic of victory in the next lifetime.

'I already knew who you were in your next lifetime . . . who you are now. It was simple. I knew what it meant. But what interested me was that I wanted to send the flowers for your death, and I was living in that time. I was somehow involved in the tragedy around the *Titanic* in as much as there was an emotional connection.'

Ann was looking perplexed. 'I knew who you were in the future, but the flowers represented a finishing of the past . . . recognition of a soul that did live. The scroll had no names and no dates. But recognition that the soul existed is important. This is just as important on the other side as it is on this earth. It is a part of your many evolutions, and unless you can be recognised through records of birth or death then what was the significance of that soul's life? Nil. Nil.'

At this point, Ann's eyes filled with tears, and I felt chills run through my body. All I could think of was Loch Cluanie, and the church that was buried beneath the water with all the records of births, deaths and marriages. Ann realised that all these souls were being reborn into lives of frustration because they could not achieve recognition for their past lives. This was a major breakthrough for us for more than one reason.

Just before Ann's visit, I happened upon a shop in the city that sold heraldry plaques. I asked about my maiden name, 'Han', not thinking that it would exist on their records because I had never had any success in tracing its origins in the past. To my surprise, the woman in the shop found it immediately. I was so thrilled to know that I would at last be learning about my heritage. The plaque was to contain the coat of arms and the meaning of the name 'Han'. I ordered the plaque and it arrived on the day that Ann had the dream about my death, and being unable to have a name or a place to send the flowers.

There are two significant details regarding the name 'Han'. One is that it can be used as either a first or last name. The given name means 'person' or 'man'. There is no firm identity attached to either of these words. It's as though the name is lost in a sea of other 'people' or 'men'. Secondly, the motto on the plaque reads 'Redeem Time'. It was so important for me to bring back the past in order to move on with my future.

This is only my story. But, there are so many others. And the importance of finding the key to your soul's frustration cannot be underestimated. The simple joy of finding peace within.

Neither Ann nor I expected to detract from the story in this way, but once we began discussing the flowers for the dead there was a strong need to peel away the layers of this mystery. There surely must have been many souls around us who understood my pain. They knew the importance of finding the missing link that would help the soul's lineage.

Before this revelation, Ann and I were discussing the *Titanic* disaster. Souls were lost and loved ones were left feeling incomplete. Ann had been dreaming about rats that were clinging to her arm. When she looked to the ground she saw half-eaten rats, but the stench was overwhelming particularly as the rats seemed to have just died. When Ann explained this to me, I then told her that I had seen rats all week outside my home. I had also smelt a stench from time-to-time and it really disturbed me. Meanwhile, there were all manner of plumbing problems in the home that week. Water was coming up through the floor, blocking the shower, and coming up through the pavers outside. Something was physically manifesting itself, and it was vital to get to the heart of the matter.

The morning after Ann and I had been writing about the communications officers on the *Titanic*, I lay in bed and couldn't get Bride, the junior officer, out of my thoughts. For two hours I struggled with a conflict raging in my mind. Eventually, a voice screamed from within, 'He was a coward!' I couldn't understand the voice in my head. I did not want to blame anyone for his or her part in the *Titanic* disaster. Finally, I got up and showered.

Ann then came downstairs and said to me, 'There's something about Bride that doesn't sit right with me.' She felt that Bride's interviews with the press did not reflect the true passage of events that night. We decided to go for a walk along the beach because Ann wanted to get rid of what she calls 'static' in order to clear her mind.

As we talked, Ann began discussing my past life. She wanted to say that something had to be resolved within me before I could be free. Ann was aware of the many personal problems I had been battling with over the years.

'Your problems are from the past ... not the present. We need to release the cause to resolve the problems.' Ann felt that it had to be done today.

It was only the previous day that I lay in meditation and said, 'I am *now* ready to release my fear.'

Ann had said that the ocean had the secrets that would set me free. But what were those secrets? And what was my fear? Ann felt that I was being torn apart in this life. She said that I was a young man in the past that had never been put to rest.

'We've already said that you were a young man, dressed in black, frantically sending messages from the *Titanic*. There *were* only two officers, and only one survived. Harold Bride was considered the hero, but Jack Phillips was never found. And he was the one who worked endlessly, trying to keep the communications open as long as possible.'

There is something worth mentioning here. I was married to a man who was in the Merchant Navy, then later worked for Marconi. His job involved the design of submarine consoles. Have I found myself in a familiar scene where the characters and situations have been repeated? I am a woman in this life, but was I a man on the *Titanic* in my last life? It was the act of writing this book that brought forward so many strange messages. The sounds of morse code that I had been getting for weeks before visiting Brisbane? Then, upon my return to Perth the signals returned and within twenty-four hours I was drawn to a book on the *Titanic*, opening it at the very page that discussed the events in the communications room as the ship sank.

So many years have been spent with mind struggles and the sense that I felt as though I had two separate natures. Always, there has been a deep longing for the sea and a yearning to 'fit in'. Where did I belong? I wrote the following poem a few months before our trip to the UK. I might add that I really didn't understand fully what I was trying to express in this verse. That is, not until now.

Twin Souls

Sadly and slowly, the twins bowed their heads
Watched the pain in their eyes as each went to bed.
Joy runs through veins of young and old alike
'Til the time steals the laughter, the sorrow and fight,
And new feelings find homes in the hearts and heads,
Of split psyches and bodies who find separate beds.

Ann and I discovered something deep within me that had been trapped, and for the first time I was given the answers to my lifelong dilemma. It is impossible to explain the sense of relief and gratitude that I felt, and the release that Ann also experienced. I could not have come to this deep and peaceful understanding on my own. Ann worked relentlessly whilst channelling information and unravelling the blockage that had hindered my psyche for so long. She told me later that she felt it was essential to complete this part of our journey before she left Perth for Brisbane. Just like the psychic tour, a door to the past would be open for only a short time. Ann knew there would not be another chance for my soul to break free from the ties of the past.

As I wrote these words, Ann looked at me curiously and asked, 'Jeanette . . . did you nearly die twice?'

Even before Ann finished her sentence, my heart was shuddering. I was frightened. Somehow, I knew that what she was going to say would terrify me. She explained that this was my third chance to live the life that my soul has always wanted to live. 'If you hadn't taken the opportunity to live your life as you wanted this time, then you would have regretted it in the years to come. It's strange, I just saw you as an elderly woman.' Ann paused for a moment and gazed into the distance. 'And you looked bitter ... too set in your ways to change, and too old to do anything about it even if you wanted to.'

Ann was referring to a major life decision that I had made early in 1999. I had an urge to change my life in 1992 when I was very ill. But I chose to remain in my situation, and the struggle with my inner conflict never left me. Finally, I decided to follow my spiritual need and created a new life for myself seven years later. Ann was trying to say that had I waited any longer then I would have been too old to reap the rewards of my new life. I always felt that I was destined to live the second half of my life in a very different way. I wanted to live my truth.

Ann said something to me that she had heard from a hypnotherapist.

'Sometimes a trauma in this life can lead us back to a trauma in a past life.'

I strongly agree with this comment. My personal experiences during and after the psychic tour seemed to catapult me out of my comfort and security zone. The emotional and physical traumas took their toll on my health, and I actually felt as though I was dragging a dead body around with me whilst writing this book. Yet, it was the act of writing this book that purged my soul. I thank her for her help and guidance.

The day following this revelation, Ann brought me three roses. One was for Jack Phillips. I had already woken to the thought that I would walk to the beach and throw a flower into the ocean in memory of that young man. He tried so hard to save so many souls. As ever, Ann and I worked in tandem, and she had the same feeling to give him a proper farewell.

The other communications officer was Harold Bride. Ann and I both had nagging feelings about this man. Without discussing these feelings, it is important first to read the following extract from one of his interviews:

'I was back in my room getting Phillips's money for him, and as I looked out the door I saw a stoker, or someone from below decks, leaning over Phillips from behind. Phillips was too busy to notice what the man was doing. The stoker was a big man, too. As you can see, I am very small. I don't know what it was I got hold of. I remembered in a flash the way Phillips had clung on—how I had to fix that lifebelt in place because he was too busy to do it. I knew that this man from below decks had his own lifebelt and should have known where to get it. I suddenly felt a passion not to let that man die a decent sailor's death. I wished he might have stretched rope or walked a plank. I did my duty. I hope I finished him. I don't know.'

Ann felt as though Bride had an inferiority complex, or 'small man's syndrome'. But he could use it to his advantage when it suited him. And whom did he finish off? Whose husband, father, brother, friend or lover was the stoker who was left to die on the sinking ship?

In another interview on 4 May 1912 with the US Senate Inquiry (Additional Testimony) before Senator William Alden Smith, Bride gives a much more controlled version of the same event. The following is an extract from that testimony.

'Leaving Mr Phillips operating, I went to our sleeping cabin, and got all our money together, returning to find a fireman or coal trimmer *gently relieving* Mr Phillips of his lifebelt. There immediately followed a general scrimmage with the three of us. I regret to say we left too hurriedly to take the man in question with us, and without a doubt he sank with the ship in the Marconi cabin as we left him.'

When questioned about the senior communications officer, Jack Phillips, Bride stated:

'As far as I can find out, he was taken on board the *Carpathia* and buried at sea from her, though for some reason the bodies of those who had died were not identified before burial from the *Carpathia*, and I can not vouch for the truth of this.'

Both statements claim that Bride had been involved with the demise of the stoker, or fireman. The first statement clearly expresses the rage of a man (Bride) incensed by what he saw, and how he had to attack the stoker, because Phillips was too busy sending communications.

However, the latter statement depicts a calmer picture of the event. In addition, Bride does not mention picking up a weapon to strike the intruder with the intent to 'finish him off'. As I was writing about this incident, I received a phone call from a young friend of mine, Stuart, in Scotland. At this point it was difficult for me to stop working, so I passed the phone over to Ann so that they could introduce themselves whilst I continued working.

As I typed the details of Phillips and his struggle, Ann wrote on a piece of paper (whilst still on the phone to Stuart) the name 'Alister', and the words 'Shot' and 'Young Man'. Two days later, I awoke in the middle of the night. I had been dreaming that I was sitting an exam. We had been asked to explain what had happened in a particular scene from a film. I wrote my answer down and innocently expected to get a good mark for my response. When I got the paper back, I didn't get any marks for my work—nil out of three. However, the others got it all right, and one man in particular who had all the details in his answer was an old work colleague of mine in real life. His name was McAlister. When Ann wrote down the name, she had spelled it Alister. This is not the normal spelling of the given name, but I was shown in a dream that there was indeed a connection to someone on the *Titanic*. However, what is more intriguing is that Ann read my notes about the dream and was convinced that I was witnessing an inquiry to do with the sinking of the *Titanic*.

She said, 'It was all a cover up. The scene from the film was actually rehearsed. You knew you were right, but everyone else's alibi was in conflict with yours. This left you helpless and bewildered. It also meant that no one would believe you.'

I realised that in my dream I was Jack Phillips. Phillips was amazed at the detail given by his 'old work colleague', Harold Bride. Jack Phillips' spirit knew the truth around the event that night in the communications room. And Bride's detailed statement was nothing like Phillips' innocent knowledge of the event.

Furthermore, Bride's statement said that Phillips 'ran aft'. He suggested that Phillips disappeared into the night. Bride then tried to help the others to lower the last collapsible boat into the water. There is a definite contrast in Bride's description of Phillips here compared to his behaviour in the communications room. Of Phillips, Bride said:

'He was a brave man. I learned to love him that night and I suddenly felt a great reverence to see him standing there sticking to his work while everyone else was raging about. I will never live to forget the work of Phillips during the last, awful fifteen minutes.'

This was a conscientious, caring man. As Bride told reporters later, when he was tired Phillips had said to him, 'You turn in boy and get some sleep.' Clearly, Phillips felt that he had a duty to both the ship and his young charge. Does this sound like a man who would 'run aft' and discharge his responsibilities?

Ann felt that there was a young man who had been shot and the look on his face was one of pure bewilderment. The gun, she said, was unusual because it was very old. By that, she meant that in 1912 it would have been at least sixty or seventy years old. Ann described the gun as long barrelled and thick. 'It fired strange bullets,' she said.

'A flare?' I suggested.

'It could have been. The hand-piece felt small and round. It was like ivory, but it was something else . . . some sort of inlay like pearl or marble. It felt comfortable. It had been used before.'

There were guns on board the *Titanic*, because as one male witness stated at the Senate Inquiry:

> 'The officers . . . had declared they'd shoot the first man that dare pass out (get into the boat).'

The question that nagged both Ann and I related to Bride's part in the assault in the communications room. He was not charged. But, a man was left to die. And what of the soul's agony? Did it deserve to wander aimlessly at the bottom of the sea? What about the family and loved ones of the man who was left to die, helpless and alone? Something did not smell right. Like the smell of dead rats, the burgeoning stench of past injustices rose to the surface. It is not for others to judge, for the soul has its own journey to continue and must deal with the inequities of its life on the earthly plane and into the next lifetime.

* * *

The whole scene in the communications room is worth questioning. Ann has a possible scenario, which I will put to you. First, Bride said that the stoker was 'a big man too', and that he (Bride) was 'very small'. Bride described how, as he looked out the doorway, he had seen the stoker trying to remove Phillips' lifebelt. The stoker, according to Bride, was leaning over Phillips from behind. Bride then grabbed something personal from his cabin. Did he then sneak up behind the stoker to attack him with the weapon (Ann felt it was a gun) and the stoker heard him? This would have been when the stoker turned on Bride, but Phillips then turned on the stoker to help his colleague. In the 'scrimmage' that followed, the gun went off accidentally injuring Jack Phillips. We have only Bride's word that he last saw Phillips on the deck. He suggested that Phillips might have been taken aboard the *Carpathia*, and that his body was buried at sea. However, as Bride stated, those bodies were not identified so he was not able to 'vouch for the truth of this'.

There is no doubt that Bride did love Jack Phillips. But when he wanted to protect him, he inadvertently caused them both great suffering. Bride died of cancer, and this tells me that something was 'eating him up'. Something that he could never speak of.

I want to go back to the night in Ann's house when I said that I felt a man was standing at my back, and Ann said that she felt the man was struggling to breathe. Bride died of lung cancer. His soul must surely have been searching for release from the pain of the past. Is there someone else on this earthly plane who has felt his guilt and anxiety? The final question is whose body was left in the cabin and remains there to this day? I feel it is Jack Phillips. That is why Ann couldn't send flowers to me when she heard of my death in her dream.

Regarding the importance of flowers, later research revealed that Jack Phillips has a memorial garden in his honour in his home of Godalming, Surrey. It is an open field of wild flowers. The secrets beneath the watery grave? Jack Phillips was my 'sea-scribe'. Born 11 April 1887—died 15 April 1912.

* * *

The story of the *Titanic* continues. One autumn night in 1999, I was sitting out on my patio when I began to smell the strong antiseptic that I associated with Sir Arthur Conan Doyle. I wanted to go inside to watch a programme that was on television called 'Her Majesty, Mrs Brown'. Yet I felt that spirit was trying to get a message to me. I decided to pick up Conan Doyle's biography and opened it at the page where he had written to the newspapers about the *Titanic* disaster. This letter was in response to George Bernard Shaw's opinion that the press had not accurately reported the *Titanic* tragedy. Bernard Shaw had accused Captain Smith of being an incompetent rather than a hero. He also suggested that the band only played on because of orders to avoid panic.

Conan Doyle was clearly distressed by these suggestions, knowing that innocent people and their families had suffered. Captain Smith had given his life, regardless of the reasons behind the disaster or his part in it. And, of the orchestra, Conan Doyle wrote:

'Finally, Mr Shaw tries to defile the beautiful incident of the band by alleging that it was the result of orders issued to avert panic. But, if it were, how does that detract either from the wisdom of the orders or from the heroism of the musicians?'

The Captain, the band that played on, and all the unfortunate ones who never had a proper burial needed to be put to rest. And the loved ones of those left behind who were never able to truly grieve their loss need to be recognised. The list is endless.

* * *

The whole *Titanic* event is of enormous importance. It wasn't until Ann came to visit me in Perth in October 2000, and we were finalising the book prior to publication, that we realised the story of the *Titanic* would not leave us. It would never rest until the silent souls under the Atlantic Ocean could find a voice to speak their truth about the tragedy of that voyage. We understood this when one night, a strange thing happened.

I had woken from a dream, as I mentioned earlier, and was writing this in my diary. I had a strong feeling that it had to do with the *Titanic*. Despite the fact that both Ann and I felt we had nearly completed this chapter, the constant messages through spirit were saying, 'Help us, don't leave us . . . you're so close.' As I lay in my bed, writing by the light of a dimmed lamp, I heard Ann come out of her bedroom. I called for her to come through, because I wanted to share my thoughts with her. Ann walked into my room, but she seemed a little incoherent and went back to bed.

The following morning, I left my notes for Ann to read before I left the house. Later that day, Ann rang me at work and told me what she felt about it. But, she also added that when she got up in the morning she saw a giant, silver spoon floating in mid-air. Ann wondered who was born with a silver spoon in their mouth? It somehow belonged to this story.

'When I walked into your room, I looked at your clock and it was 3:05am. And it scared me. You know when you hear about someone who has died and the clock stops? That's what the feeling was. Something was frozen in time. But, it wasn't the death of a person ... it was the death of the truth. It frightened me. I couldn't change it. I knew it would be buried for a long, long time. And there wasn't a thing I could do about it. By April 2012 the true story will be known.'

Ann picked up that there was a problem with the water pumps on the ship. The young men who were left on duty that night did not know how to operate them, or forgot to turn them on in their rush to escape. Had they found time to do this, the water pumps could have kept the ship afloat a lot longer.

Later that day, Ann wrote three pages of automatic writing. The following transcript will be broken in to smaller parts, and each section will be explained in full. The reader might also be able to pick up something else in Ann's writing that will be useful.

You were also on that ship (Ann). You were seen by many, but questioned by few.

Ann was involved with the *Titanic* story at the time, but not actually **on** the *Titanic*. It was as though she was somehow recording the events on shore after the tragedy. She saw something familiar to her at that time, something about the bodies that she recognised as being very important.

Because yours was a job to do, you did it well, condemned so many all to hell.

The above statement reflects the restraint that Ann felt in speaking up for others. If she kept going and going then somebody would believe what she had seen.

You have kept the flame to pass it on, don't allow history to linger on. You did your job and paid the price—so it goes with the privileged race.

Hence the image of that large silver spoon. Ann had recorded information during the *Titanic* era.

However, those who were privileged by birth or status had their opinions aired, and others struggled to tell their version of the event. It is time to bring the truth to the surface. The rich and powerful can't keep the truth suppressed indefinitely.

A judge you have been, a judge you were.

She got the stories from people, and then decided what and how they should be told.

The stories abound of what was in store—
nothing of truth for history to store.

So many fantasies about the sinking of the *Titanic*—nothing is really true.

Her maiden voyage was dammed to begin,
the spinnakers were raised for all within.
The ship of shame was about to sail, so
weak and thin ... much too frail.

This ship was not structurally strong enough ... Lightweight new metal, gives room to store (munition). Spinnakers raised as though going in to battle, this ship was built to deceive ... carrying illegal goods within the cavities— she was torn apart from without and within.

Not only was there external damage from the iceberg, but there was also an explosion inside the ship where the coal was kept. She was built for money, yet not enough was spent to build her.

> *The sea swallows up, those that choose to ignore. The innocents do pay, it evens the score. Yet in the end, they will all be set free to walk the land with you and me. Freedom for everyone, all classes and creeds ... no longer the gypsies condemned to the sea.*

The above states that they were warned the structure was not sound enough. Naive people trusted the powers that be that this would work. The day that documents will show the truth of this is coming, and innocent workmanship can no longer be blamed.

> *The torch will rise to show the truth, you, Ann survived to see it—the truth.*

The light you shed on this story will bring, in time, evidence to the surface. The truth will prevail.

> *The judgement is done, the souls will emerge from their place in history's water bed.*

The proper death toll will be known when the cover-ups are exposed.

The key to your future is as it has always been, to cleanse the guilty and damn the clean.

As before, Ann will always seek to report the facts. Truths as they are, not how some wish them to be seen.

For reverse is the truth as history will show, and get on with the job as you well know.

The truth must be told at all cost, otherwise lies breed more lies and the truth does get lost.

You have the guts to stand your point, no howling winds will change your course. We speak as one and one for all, enlighten those so-called souls that struggle with the cause.

This time Ann is in a position to take on the challenge, as she is now her own boss ... and is able to show those that are looking for the answers where to find them. However, she must start within.

The growth you will find will expand many lands, and for god's sake woman—give Jeanette a hand! Her transformation is almost complete, so at night she will be able to sleep.

More and more people will start to seek out the truth, for the past holds the key to our present lives. Ann must help those closest, until they can release their past fears, to find the strength within.

The love she will have (Jeanette) from the pain of the past will teach her new strengths that forever will last.

The knowing of where I came from only strengthens and gives a better understanding of myself that will never diminish and will only become stronger.

But her footsteps will go deep into the sand that will reach across many lands.

The path you both have chosen will help many, for her (Jeanette) stories will be able to carry the weary when they don't have the strength to carry themselves (like St Christopher).

On and on I could forever go. But that's not my duty as you and I know. We could continue to talk forever, but it's not for me to tell you. You have free will and know what to do. The answer is deep, deep inside, and you know how to make it rise. You know how and what you need to do— your destiny! In love and light, Danny (the spirit who gave this information).

But, there was something else. Ann had felt that there was someone on the *Titanic* who held secrets to the past. These secrets had to do with the Ripper murders and freemasonry. Whatever was hidden within that ship must be exposed, and this ought to be done fearlessly.

Once again, I quote from Michael Coren's book in which Sir Arthur Conan Doyle is quoted as saying:

> 'For when a man does a thing secretly and anonymously he does not enclose literature that will lead to his detection.'

For example, the statements Bride provided to the inquiry the month following the disaster did not mention his 'finishing off' of the stoker. And what of the passengers who did not survive? Why were so many hurriedly buried at sea unidentified? Where are the records to show their belongings? What was the *Titanic* carrying other than its passengers and normal cargo?

The secrets beneath the watery grave needed a voice. And the voice will be the literature that is detected on land. For when the *Titanic* docked at a port there would be a ship's manifest for payment of goods. Ann knew that only time would tell if anything else would come our way from spirit. She had told me in Brisbane that there was some follow on from the *Titanic* and it had to do with a wealthy American family. She talked of Robert Kennedy and Marilyn Monroe.

'Something will come through,' she said.

We could only wait and see.

14

Ancient Rituals and the Druids

21 October 1998

Today we drove to Wales and were told about the Isle of Anglesey which is the original home of the Druids. We were told of their regular annual festivals in the north and south of Wales.

The Druids were Celtic shamans, or wise men who were spiritually and politically powerful within their culture. They had long apprentice-ships of approximately twenty years and were learned scholars. Much of their time was spent alone in search of profound spiritual experiences. They advised their kings and acted as a bridge between the spiritual and material worlds. Poets and visionaries, they were upheld in their society as well respected sages.

The Romans invaded the island of Anglesey in AD 60, and wiped out both the island and the Druids. But a mysterious discovery in 1984 resurrected the memory of the Druids in a powerful way. A peat cutter in the south of Manchester, England, found the body of a well-preserved man. The tannins in the bog had mummified the body, and experts gleaned through blood tests that the man was a Celt, and they dated the body back to AD 60. Other investigations revealed that he was a Druid and quite possibly a Prince. He was wearing a fox-fur armband and this denoted nobility. However, his death had been violent and was more than likely sacrificial. The 'Death of a Prince' and ritual practices seemed to echo throughout our journey.

Later, we were taken to Bewtsy-cood, which had a very soft energy. The chapel within the glen of trees is a heritage building on an island in the middle of the River Conway. There was an intense privacy about the place. Locals would speak in their native tongue, and a sense of secrecy imbued the forest area.

In writing about this part of our journey I had a strong feeling that there was a symbolic relationship between the ancient Druid practices and the Jack-the-Ripper murders. I found one of Ann's

automatic writings which I felt was important to
include in this section of the book. Written by her
on 29 October 1998 in London, it is a description
of a ritual practice which appears to involve Prince
Eddy. I say this because Ann channelled some very
vital information which supports this on the same
night in our London hotel. I have her channelling
on a tape. You can read the full transcript of this
tape toward the end of the book. But, for now this
is the automatic writing she channelled and gave
to me on the trip.

*He came from a place beyond the trees, he
was not alone . . . all about him was quiet.
He knew he could be seen at any time, but
that did not distract him from the purpose
at hand. His quest was quite clear, get the
job done and then relinquish his fear.*

*The power of the soul is not to pass on
without at least seeing how the other one
lived. Thus you will see into the future.
Enjoy the kill; receive the rewards . . . regret
is not for now but for later. He walked
away with his head held high; those in the
know sang praise. Little did they fear the
outcome that would be, the pigs in the
wood would see clear. They came so close
to catching him, but he alone was not guilty*

of sin. The clan were proud for in their
wake was the future king that could create,
he bore his soul and they gave the score.

This was to have enormous significance in unveiling the mystery of the young Prince's involvement with the Freemasons and the Jack-the-Ripper murders. Ann had already stated that she felt he was not the only one, and this came through repeatedly.

Before leaving for the trip, a friend of mine invited me to a lecture on the Druids at the University of Western Australia. I nearly declined, but for some reason I went along. The Chief of the Druids was visiting from Britain and I found his talk intriguing.

He explained through the use of myth how the Goddess was feared and revered amongst the Druids. A male sect, they saw that the power of the Goddess was in her ability to create. She created life and the cycle continued. This ancient order with its many rituals and practices in some way reflected the need for the rebellious group of young Freemasons to achieve a sense of power. The victims of Jack the Ripper appeared to be the unfortunate ones who were chosen to satisfy the heady, primal wants of this new, rebellious sect.

We were in Wales for two days and we managed to make two very important connections the following day when we were in the small village of Llangollen.

15

Secrets Found in Books and Art

22 October 1998

The Café Bookshop in Llangollen, Wales, is said to have some of the oldest books in Britain. This was not difficult to believe. The old, stacked shelves held many books of interest. I picked up a book about Queen Victoria and read a passage regarding Prince Eddy. In 1890 his father, the Prince of Wales, expressed his concern about the young Prince. He deemed that a 'good, sensible wife' was urgently needed. The Prince's future and education were a matter of anxiety and his Secretary was to attend to these matters urgently 'for the good of the country'. I took note of this for Ann who was scouring the bookshelves for something on May of Teck.

I could hear young Christine's voice whispering excitedly. She was with Ann when they came upon the book *Queen Mary*, written by James Pope-Hennessy. Ann was thrilled. She didn't want to devour the whole book, merely glean a few facts that would shape our discoveries and confirm some of the information she had been picking up.

Whilst Ann was purchasing this book and chatting to the sales assistant I had an urge to find something on the social life in Victorian times. My hand fell upon a book about Oscar Wilde. This was the first connection. I simply wrote in my notebook, 'Oscar Wilde . . . Decadence'. I felt that there was something to be followed up here regarding all the socialising of Oscar Wilde and Prince Eddy. Ann wanted to know when Prince Eddy stopped socialising. She talked to me of researching newspapers of the day for clues to the Prince's movements. All of this would be done on our return to Australia. Secrets would be revealed in the most abstract manner. Ann would go back to find truths hidden in fiction and art.

After leaving Llangollen, we travelled to Ludlow where we had the opportunity to do some sightseeing and shopping. But I couldn't resist going into a bookshop to scour the section on Victorian England. I found a book and, as usual, it fell open at the required page. It was a snippet about May of Teck and how Prince Eddy had died only one month after their engagement. This was becoming fascinating reading, but I could feel the eyes of the shop owner burning through me. Abi appeared, and I asked her to shield me whilst I continued reading about May being brought up in England. It made me think about Ann's regression, and the little girl who watched as the other children played. How she had tried to talk to the therapist but could not speak English, and how she felt that she was not 'part' of that family. And, in many ways, this reserved and intelligent woman never was a real part of that family. I could hardly wait to tell Ann of my findings.

Finally, we boarded the bus and headed back to our hotel in Wales. It was very old and some of the rooms were quite small, but it had real character and a surprising host was awaiting our company that night!

We had arranged to get together in someone's room to do a little psychic development. As we walked into the room, several of us could feel a presence. It was hard to describe, but Ann immediately said it was an older gentleman who was a little the worse for wear because he liked a tipple.

'He's quite harmless,' Ann said. 'He's just happy to see all these women in the same room.'

Chris glared at Ann. 'Well, I felt someone pinch

my bottom. And I was wondering which one of you would do that! But when I looked around there was nobody there.'

We were meant to be studying psychometry (picking up information by holding objects), but it must have been the cheeky presence of this old man that had us in fits of laughter. No matter what we did we always ended up laughing uncontrollably, but Ann noticed that Linda seemed a little bit disturbed by the spirit around us.

Later, when talking to Linda, it was clear she feared that perhaps the spirit had a connection to her past, and this had touched a sensitive area. But this was not the case. He was not connected in any way to Linda. Rather, his jovial energy was recharging our weary batteries after such an intensive trip.

Suddenly, during the laughter, Ann held up her hand and without looking signalled for us all to be silent. She was sitting on the bed staring at young Christine. Ann had been talking to Christine and asked her if she could feel anything. Then she noticed the familiar signs of someone slipping into trance. Christine was not in a deep trance, but she was at the level where she could hear what was being said whilst responding to her current reality. Also, her voice had changed. This is another indication that a person has regressed into a past life. Ann asked her who she was.

'I'm a nurse.' Christine's voice was soft and low.

Ann then asked her questions about the era and her duties. Christine was very clear and accurate with her responses. She was disappointed, because she wanted to help the soldiers in the war and her father would not allow her to go because she was a woman.

She knew that she was an excellent nurse and was capable of performing her duties in the battle-field. Her resentment was obvious. This shocked me for one reason only. And it had nothing to do with Christine going into trance.

It concerned Sir Arthur Conan Doyle. I had recently read his biography, which I bought in Edinburgh. Conan Doyle was a doctor and whilst he was too old for service in the Boer War he was still able to participate in his medical capacity. It chills me now to write about it, because the medium that had gone into trance in my home in Australia could smell a strong antiseptic that was used in hospitals long ago. The first words she spoke were, 'My name is Arthur.' Afterwards, she said the smell was so overpowering that it made her feel quite nauseous.

There was another psychic present at that time. She provided the medium with water after she came out of trance and told us both what she had seen during the medium's trance. She described a man sitting by the beds of soldiers and writing for their families back home. 'It's Conan Doyle!' she said.

This man had great respect and appreciation for those who helped the wounded during the Boer War. In Michael Coren's book *Conan Doyle*, he is quoted as writing:

> 'In the very worst of it two nursing sisters appeared among us, and never shall I forget what angels of light they appeared, or how they nursed those poor boys, swaddling them like babies and meeting every want with gentle courage. Thank God, they both came through safe.'

Conan Doyle had a close and tragic association with those who had lost their loved ones in war for seventeen years later his son, Kingsley, died on Armistice Day in 1917. The young soldier fought his last battle whilst Conan Doyle was spreading his beliefs on spiritualism.

* * *

When our tour ended I stayed in the UK for another month, but Ann went back to Australia and began investigating the murders in more detail.

It was shortly after I got back to Perth that she rang and told me that she'd started reading Oscar Wilde's famous novel, *The Picture of Dorian Gray*. Ann was very excited about this latest discovery, and I was glad that she had stumbled on it. She said that she had no idea why she began reading it, but once she had glanced through the book she became acutely aware that the shocking truth of the past lay in Wilde's words.

It appeared that clues were hidden within the story that included all the main characters at the time of the Ripper murders. Like Chinese dolls, there were layers of the Victorian underworld being revealed one after the other. What we found will be revealed to you shortly.

16

Escaping the Floods

23 October 1998

The Welsh leg of our journey involved a lot of travelling and sightseeing by coach. This was a quiet part of our tour. That is, until the heavy rain started.

It rained heavily during the night in Llandindrod. None of us realised how torrential the rain had been until the following morning. As we boarded the coach there was talk of the floods and it was anticipated that it would get worse.

As we drove to Caerphilly there were a lot of police on the road in front of us. They gestured for our bus to stop. It appeared that there were serious problems on the roads leaving Wales. The water had swelled to an alarming degree. There had been such excitement on the journey that we never stopped to consider the possibility of problems such as this one. What would happen if we could not get out of Wales? We had learned so much. Surely it wouldn't all come to an end now? A creeping sense of anxiety washed over me. But we were lucky. There was another road we could take to avoid the rushing waters. I began to realise in a small way how trapped those souls on the *Titanic* must have felt. With no escape, and only the knowledge that one was at the mercy of the divine, it must have been a living nightmare.

I must commend the patience and endurance of our driver for he drove many miles under some very dangerous conditions. Meanwhile, we watched villagers from the bus as they swept the water out of their sandstone cottages. The sandbags had done little to deter the incessant flooding. We were very fortunate not to have been caught in this deluge.

The police redirected our coach driver and we took an alternative route. As we drove I watched the red, gushing waters follow us along the roadside. It was as though we had made a narrow escape from the harsh, Welsh countryside. On our way to the Brecon Beacons Mountains we could see the army ahead of us. Clearly, the situation was still serious and by now we were desperate to get away from the relentless floods.

We journeyed on, and as we passed the village of Aberfan the tour director told us that it was the week of the anniversary of the 1966 Aberfan disaster. I remembered this tragic event. Primary school children were buried alive when the land slid on top of the village school. As a primary school student myself at that time it was not difficult to feel the pain of those children. I had written a poem dedicated to them. And here I was thirty-two years later, looking down on the village that I had only heard about on television. It was remarkable that our psychic tour took us to the spot where those young souls died tragically.

There were to be no goodbyes from mothers, fathers, families or friends. More and more, we were made aware of the grief that lay hidden beneath graves of water and soil. How could we ignore the meaning of this journey?

Spirits cry to be heard, to be recognised as part of this world so that they may pass through to the other side. If they are unable to do this then the souls are forever bound to the earth plane. It is hard for souls to move on when family members and friends are still holding on to them. People do not recognise that there is a need for them to get to the other side. The souls need to do this in order to look back on the life they have just left.

Ann has taught spiritual and psychic development for many years and she shared these insights with me. Ann explained that the souls are reunited with their Spiritual Guide or Guardian Angel, for they chose to work and walk their path with that divine being as 'equals'. Ann always makes one point very clear and it is this. We did not come back to earth this lifetime to work with or under a 'master'. That would surely make us slaves. Our guidance comes from highly developed divine souls that have completed their earth's journeys. They are now working on the other side as tutors. Together, they can see whether or not they have accomplished all that they chose to achieve this lifetime. Some souls are not ready to accept that they have passed on whilst others wish to be released quickly.

The soul only knows whether it has learned its lessons this lifetime when it reaches the other side. For this is a partnership between a divine being (your Spiritual Guide or Guardian Angel) and the soul. Both parties must achieve their respective lessons. Whilst sitting on the coach I thought of the expression, 'when two worlds collide'. I believe they blend. Our world is every bit as real as the world on the other side. They are as one.

The tour director interrupted my thoughts when he announced that we were on our way to Bath.

Here we would see the Roman Baths, which were believed to have healing powers for the souls in this world and the next. Could anything be more poetic? The hot springs of the Roman Baths were in sharp contrast to the cold, rushing blood-red waters we had left behind in Wales. When the Romans discovered the hot springs they saw them as the border between mortal man and the immortal gods. This was not a natural phenomenon to them. The head of a statue of Minerva was found whilst digging the foundations for a building to be built on the Roman Baths. Minerva was the Roman goddess of the waters. In Celtic myth there is also a goddess of waters named Sulis.

Minerva *was* the Roman goddess of war, wisdom and the arts, but in Bath she is equated with the Celtic goddess Sulis. Sulis had healing powers and was a deity, hence the name of the Temple, Sulis-Minerva.

We were shown the Temple of Sulis-Minerva. The Temple Courtyard was a place of sacrifice. The augur told the future using the liver of a sacrificed animal and by looking at the stars.

All of this reflected the activity of the Druids and the Freemasons. What is also interesting is that the Baths were discovered around 1890. This paralleled the era of the Ripper murders. So, even though we were learning about the hidden past of the Romans some two thousand years ago, it still fitted neatly into the time frame we were dealing with on the psychic tour.

Today was one of relaxation and reflection, but the messages remained clear. We were still dealing with the same themes of death, power and rebirth. Yet, there was one special addition to this list, and it was that of healing. Healing is indeed possible. The goddess Minerva may have had the power to kill, but Sulis also had the wisdom to heal. This has to be of significance for the tortured souls who must move on.

We boarded the bus just as twilight was falling. We drove by Royal Avenue, and near the bandstand a squirrel ran through the autumn leaves. The light continued to fade as we drove past the lamp-lit house where Jane Austen had lived. The warmth from the glow stretched upward and onto the lattice high above the home. Peace and gentleness filled the air that night. We needed the tranquillity of this day for the tour had claimed our energies somewhat. The healing waters of Bath offered time for reflection, and time for renewal.

17

Secrets and Lies

24 October 1998

'For when a man does a thing secretly and anonymously he does not enclose literature that will lead to his detection.'

I was compelled to write this in my notepad before we left our hotel in Bristol to visit Glastonbury Abbey, Clovelly and Tintagel. Conan Doyle's quote refers to the tampering of evidence and psychic phenomena. I took the trouble to copy the quote in my journal and knew that it would somehow find its place in this book.

* * *

On 20 December 1999, I spoke to Ann by phone regarding a personal matter. Just before I hung up she asked, 'Have you written the section on Tintagel yet?'

I thought for a moment and said, 'I haven't checked my notes yet, but I think it must be coming up very soon.'

Ann explained that she was picking up something 'not quite right' about Tintagel.

Located on the north coast of Cornwall, Tintagel's history includes the legend of King Arthur and the Knights of the Round Table. King Athur's adviser was Merlin who was allegedly a wizard or shaman. His powers were similar to those of the Druids. On the day we visited Tintagel we were taken to a cliff top which faced the ruins of King Arthur's castle. The wind was so strong that I had to make a great effort to force my body forward towards the edge of the cliff. There was a temptation to get as close to the edge as possible.

A storm was building and as I looked across at the ravaged castle I felt a sense of defeat around the blackened, sea-washed structure. The tales of sorcery and manipulation that engulfed King Arthur's reign easily captured my imagination as I stood amidst the tempestuous surroundings.

When Ann spoke to me by phone she said she saw a body, but the clothing was that of this generation. Someone was murdered and there was some sort of a cover up. She would visit me the next day and start channelling for more information.

Suddenly, Ann's voice changed, and in a rather authoritarian voice she said, 'Jeanette . . . LISTEN! I've got a man here and a really strong smell of antiseptic. It's Conan Doyle. And he's saying that you're picking up something, but only getting part of the message. I'll leave it with you. Just ask what it is you need to know.'

Well, now I knew why I was constantly drawn to Conan Doyle's biography. I hadn't smelt the antiseptic for some months, but clearly he was trying desperately to come through. It was time for me to fine-tune my psychic awareness to interpret the message.

Earlier I mentioned that communication with spirit requires a different sort of language and it's not always straightforward. This was one of those times!

I returned to my notes and realised that today was the day I would indeed be writing about Tintagel. It never failed to amaze me how perfectly in sequence Ann and I were whilst collaborating on this book.

The following day Ann arrived. We were looking at the legend of King Arthur and surrounding myths. Ann could not shake the feeling that all was not as it seemed at Tintagel.

The legend of the Holy Grail depicts a chalice. However, Ann kept getting a scroll.

'There was no chalice,' she said. 'It was the written word, and I feel it's written on something like soft leather.' It was the written word that had to be continued, Ann said later. 'Something about keeping the image alive of the King or Christ, or whoever was considered godlike.'

Ann looked serious and continued, 'It was something that had been created, and those around the leader were responsible for this "new law" that was to have the power of life and death over others.' Ann felt that the leader or King would not have known what was going on around him regarding this new written law.

Going deeper into this mystery, Ann said she felt that it symbolised how people were ruled and controlled by fear. Keeping a story alive that was created and mythologised did this.

The question is, how is this all linked to Jack the Ripper? The answer lies in the Royal Family. Keeping the tradition and power of the Monarchy alive meant that knowledge had to be tampered with or withheld.

Examples of this are available to the public. It is no secret that Queen Victoria's papers and journals were either destroyed or transcribed on her death by her daughter, Princess Beatrice.

Ultimately, they were nothing more than fabrications of the original text. This also applied to the papers of Prince Albert Consort and Prince Albert Victor, or Eddy as he was known.

Prince Eddy's brother, Prince George, was very distressed by this action, but he was unable to preserve the writings of the Queen as she had clearly ordered her daughter to perform this task immediately upon her death.

It is timely to quote Conan Doyle once more.

'For when a man does a thing secretly and anonymously he does not enclose literature that will lead to his detection.'

We now have to question all that was *not shown* at the time of the Ripper murders themselves, and at the Ripper inquest. The files were sealed for one hundred years, but when the day arrived that they were to be made available it was discovered that many had either been tampered with or were missing. Again, this is factual evidence that was detailed in later reports. Furthermore, one autopsy report was completely missing. And Queen Victoria's morbid fascination with death cannot be ignored here either. It was imperative that she knew all the details of the Ripper inquest from Sir William Gull, her Physician-in-Ordinary.

'Oh what a tangled web we weave, when first
we practise to deceive.'

When King Arthur died his body was taken to
Avalon to be magically healed. Avalon is another
name for the Welsh Otherworld. This man, who
was a so-called 'child of destiny', was then mythologised by people and became their saviour. Excal-
ibur, the sword of truth, has been used to cut
through truths in order to present lies. On King
Arthur's tomb are the words, *Here lies Arthur,
king that was, king that shall be*. But, the myth
of the man did not survive his death. His kingdom
was weakened, and his hatred for his own nephew,
Modred, ended in battle. He was indeed human,
and his power only transitory.

This theme goes back to the story of Christ as
it was written in the Bible, but has been manip-
ulated by each generation to fabricate further the
saintliness of an ordinary man. Christ was an ordinary man who was a visionary and a healer.

Looking back at Prince Eddy's death, there were
many eulogies for a young man who in the public's
eye did not contribute anything of significance to
society.

Many Royal households were aware of the
Prince's reputation, and consequently refused
the proposal of marriage into the most powerful

family of Great Britain. Queen Victoria was well aware of the young man's decadent lifestyle, and she knew that he could tarnish the Monarchy's image and possibly destroy all that she had worked so hard to build and control. Ann felt sure that it was impossible for the Queen not to be aware of the Prince's illnesses. Yet, she was still prepared to marry him off to some poor, hapless woman.

The Private Secretary to the Prince of Wales, Sir Francis Knollys, once wrote:

> 'I ask again, who is it tells the Queen these things?'

He was writing to the Queen's Private Secretary, Lord Ponsonby, in December 1891. Ponsonby was a servant to the Queen for many years. She baffled everyone with her inside knowledge regarding the people within the Royal circle and political arena. Her need to pry into the lives of those around her was essential if she was to protect the image of the Monarchy.

The public did not really know Prince Eddy except for the carefully manufactured reports that could be read in the newspapers of the day. He could walk among them and they wouldn't know who he was. As I wrote this I mentioned to Ann that she had a piece of automatic writing from the trip that said something similar. I asked her if she would mind me including it at this point. She agreed, and to our amazement we found that it had been written on 24 October 1998—the very day that we were at Tintagel. Ann wrote:

Today is a day you will see no more. The future king will be seen to make the score. The towns will bring joy for all to see. The creature of night walks among thee.

It fitted in perfectly for this part of our journey. Again, spirit works in the most incredible manner to ensure that all details are brought together.

But, first of all let us look closely at the words Ann received. '*Today is a day you will see no more.*' Ann got the words 'lost innocence'. Something would be changed forever because of a single deed. Then, '*The future king will be seen to make the score.*' Outwardly, this appeared that the Prince had attempted his initiation into some Freemason ritual yet it suggests that he didn't fully complete the ritual. Ann was picking up that his colleagues were spreading propaganda saying that he was successful when in fact someone else had to finish off the initiation ceremony. And what did that initiation involve? Ann was getting the word 'squeamish'.

It was as though his associates accepted the responsibility for his lack of cooperation. For the sake of honour they would cover up for his cowardice. Ann then began talking about his ambivalence towards these rituals.

'There was all the talk about participating in these occult matters. Yet, if he wasn't smoking opium, or at least under the influence of some mind altering drug, he really wasn't interested in any of the young men's wild fantasies.'

The Prince first came into contact with a splinter group whilst at Trinity College which he attended from 1883–1885. This is where he met his tutor, James Kenneth Stephen, who was a member of the homosexual society known as the Apostles. Stephen was only five years older than the Prince. Their relationship was subject to rumours of intimacy between tutor and pupil.

I feel urged to revisit Ann's earlier psychic awareness when we stood within the walls of Trinity Church in Oxford. She was picking up two young men who seemed inseparable. One was highly intelligent and took on the responsibility for the younger student. Although we were dealing with another era at the beginning of this journey, we crossed a barrier into the nineteenth century where the circumstances were the same. For in spiritual realms time is infinite and not linear.

'*The towns will bring joy for all to see.*' Ann was getting that it was a feast day or public holiday in England when the initiation took place. '*The creature of night walks among thee.*' This means that the person could walk among the crowds and no one would know who he was or feel threatened by him. One of the Ripper murders took place on a bank holiday. The murdered body of Ripper victim, Martha Tabram, was found on Tuesday, 7 August 1888.

* * *

I don't wish to leave Ann's first feelings about Tintagel left unexplained. She had seen a dead body in modern day clothing in the old castle. She wasn't sure if the man had been murdered or if it was symbolic. As we began discussing this, Ann had a sudden insight. She clapped her hands together and said, 'Who's being sacrificed today in the Monarchy?'

Please do not take the word sacrifice literally. Ann was getting a feeling that someone was deemed not suitable to be the future King. This is where a sacrifice must be made in order for the Monarchy to continue. It also symbolised that any modern view might be deemed as threatening, and dealt with accordingly.

History shows us that the Monarchy has feared how it is perceived by the masses. Tradition and stability are cornerstones of the Firm, and have been considered imperative for its survival. However, the death of Diana, Princess of Wales saw the Royal Family forced to change its attitude. This saved the Crown and kept the masses aligned with the Royals, albeit tenuously.

* * *

The same day we visited Tintagel, we also visited a little village called Clovelly. Here, a woman called Christine Hamlin tried to control and secure the village's heritage. She also wanted her husband to take her name in marriage. It is not difficult to see the comparison between this woman and the rigid adherence to principle of Queen Victoria, and today's Monarchy. Clovelly, as I perceived it, presented in microcosm the power and control of the Monarchy at large.

* * *

Ann feels that there is only one more reigning monarch for Great Britain. When Ann talked of a sacrifice within the Royal Family she was referring to the following; the next King will not be

Prince Charles. Rather, he will have to sacrifice his seat on the throne for one of his sons.

Significantly, the past has shown that the eldest son has not always successfully ascended the throne. For example, Prince Albert Victor died in 1892, the reign of King Edward VII lasted only nine years from 1901 to 1910 and King Edward VIII abdicated in 1936.

The question arises, how has this affected the lives of these men through generations who have never lived to satisfy their destiny? Herein lies the true meaning of the word 'sacrifice' referred to by Ann. She saw the Monarchy as becoming similar in role to the other European Royal houses. That is to say, they will marry whomever they wish. The gradual demise of the mystical quality attached to royalty over the next ten years means that they can no longer hide behind the walls of secrecy.

18

The Lady in Black

25 October 1998

As I awoke this morning, I saw a vision of an elderly woman wearing a long, black skirt and a black shawl. She looked as though she came from the early nineteenth century. The impression was strong and stayed with me for some time.

We visited St Ives and Penzance, and stood at the end of the earth, Land's End. Looking out to sea there was a sense of clarity, yet sadness lingered in the air. Here, there was nowhere to hide.

Ann had given me her book on May of Teck to read. I had been reading the section where Prince Eddy had met his fate at Sandringham on 14 January 1892 only six days after his twenty-eighth birthday.

The first week of January 1892 was bitterly

cold. The Sandringham property had been chosen by Prince Albert Consort because it was 'very inaccessible', and he had hoped that it would thwart the 'pleasure loving tendencies' of his son, the Prince of Wales. However, its remoteness did not stop the Prince from indulging in late night parties and playing practical jokes.

I was able to accept most of the material I read, but I then felt uncomfortable whilst reading the following extract about Prince Eddy's death.

'On the 13th he was delirious shouting "at the top of his voice" about his regiment, his horses and his brother officers, talking wildly of Lord Salisbury and the Lord Randolph Churchill, and of how much he loved his grandmother the Queen.'

The whole scene sounded so chaotic, frightening and unreal that the next piece of information completely contradicted the severity of the situation.

Queen Victoria wanted to leave for Sandringham urgently, but the Prince of Wales' incredulous response was that he 'begged his mother by telegram not to journey down to Sandringham'.

The Prince's reasoning was that the whole party was suffering so badly from influenza, and the

Queen should not be subject to any possible virus. However, those who attended the family party had done so despite their existing ailments. Furthermore, the Royal Physician did not accompany the Prince of Wales and the future King to Sandringham. A local doctor, Dr Manby, was called in to assist the dying Prince. On 11 January, Dr Francis Larkin, the Physician-in-Ordinary to the Prince of Wales, arrived to assist Dr Manby.

I explained how I felt to Ann as we sat in the tearooms in St Ives. 'I can actually see a cloud over my head.' Ann told me to close the book and leave it alone for a while.

'We're picking up so much psychic energy,' Ann said, '. . . too much. We need to concentrate on what we're getting rather than all the written information too. Otherwise, we'll be thrown off balance.'

Ann explained that the purest channelling will always come from the soul itself, and any external information is merely human perception. There are reasons for the latter, but in general the author needs to satisfy some outer demand. In this way, stories can be told to glorify an image.

Both Ann and I felt Prince Eddy had a glorified image of Lord Randolph Churchill. His name was one of the few that Prince Eddy had called out in his delirious state. Churchill enjoyed the adulation, but Ann felt that it became 'tiresome'. Known as 'Randy' in some circles, he was a member of the 'fast' set. He also suffered from syphilis which he contracted at an early age and this eventually led to his death.

The Prince of Wales was the most prominent person within this group of high-powered men, and Ann felt that Prince Eddy was made to join his father on certain occasions.

'It's almost as though his father didn't feel that Prince Eddy fitted his perception of a "real man". He was getting too much feedback and gossip that his son's interests were in other areas. Apart from his sexuality, the Prince of Wales was concerned about the young Prince taking drugs.'

Ann explained that she felt the father did not agree with the drug taking, but he could accept alcohol and womanising.

'At the same time he was so jealous of his son. He hated him because Queen Victoria showed so much love for her grandson. It's strange,' Ann continued thoughtfully, 'it's as though she felt she wouldn't have him for long. She felt the gentleness in him, because she could see herself in him at times . . . the confused mind . . . they both at times heard voices . . . he must have talked to her at some time about it.'

Ann grew silent, and was completely unaware

of her surroundings. Then, she softly said, ' . . . as she talks to her daddy.'

Ann looked at me. I said, 'But Queen Victoria was only a year old when her father died?'

Ann said, 'That's what I got . . . as she talks to her daddy. The Queen was very psychic. She was getting messages, but she didn't understand them. And, she kept a lot to herself for fear of being removed.'

Ann felt the Queen had seen too many of her family members fall ill to traumas. She said that those traumas were not always correctly diagnosed. I then shared with Ann my feelings about Queen Victoria's astrology chart. This woman must surely have suffered from a great deal of uncertainty and confusion about her own identity. She was so psychic that she was 'picking up' constantly from not only those on the other side, but those around her.

Ann was still gazing into the distance. Then she said, 'It's as though she had always known she was going to be Queen, and she would never allow herself to lose sight of her destiny.'

The insight into the relationship between Queen Victoria and Prince Eddy gave Ann a great deal of satisfaction. She at last understood why Prince Eddy's father was so cruel to his own flesh and blood with his constant taunting.

'What amazes me,' she continued, 'is that Queen Victoria had such a fondness for Prince Eddy, but there was no question where her loyalties lay when it came to the protection of the throne.'

Queen Victoria wanted to make contact with her deceased husband, but Ann said she was unable to do so. She could talk to her father, but she doubted her abilities to communicate with Prince Albert Consort.

This brings us to the Queen's relationship with Mr John Brown. The feeling we had about their friendship was not one of romance, but something much deeper. In the book, *Life at the Court of Queen Victoria*, we learn that Brown was,

'supposed to be a medium and was able to put the Queen Victoria in touch with the spirit of Prince Albert.'

And, how did Brown cross the Queen's path? He literally crossed her path so that he could save her life. This divine intervention was no coincidence. For this man who helped the Queen laugh again after her many years of grieving was able to give her confirmation that her husband was indeed still with her and keeping her safe. The Prince of Wales detested Brown because he saw that a higher love

THE LADY IN BLACK

existed between his mother and her faithful servant. He could not relate to it, or come close to understanding it. His ego and lifestyle meant that he related only to material pleasures, but his birth did not automatically entitle him to receive something he could not give himself. This love transcended any earthly feelings. His anger was eventually made manifest after the Queen's death when he destroyed all the statuettes she had placed in John Brown's memory.

It is now timely to remember Mr John Brown as a medium that served the Queen, and as a soul who fulfilled his destiny on this earthly plane. Love comes in many forms, and this deep and affectionate connection was one that was of the spirit for the spirit. The Queen's late husband could not have chosen a more beautiful soul.

19

Breakthrough

26 October 1998

The lid of the door is about to explode,
where it's to land no-one will know. But the
future will see it was not theirs to hide, for
the souls that were kept deep inside. They
will have their say and judgement will be
done. Freedom and happiness for everyone,
all their names will be cleared pure of sin.

Ann channelled this automatic writing today,
26 October 1998. At the same time another
woman on the tour, also called Ann, received
automatic writing which talked of Prince Eddy's
death and the akashic records. She handed me the
writings during breakfast in the hotel. The following are extracts from her notes.

Tell Ann what happened to the king in the night . . . he had to succumb to the malaise, **the third time was right** *. . . they couldn't see past him in terrible plight . . . they helped him come through with opium at night. It's all there for her to view, just open the akashic and all will come through . . .*

We left Plymouth today and were headed towards Dartmoor, Stonehenge and Salisbury. On the coach, Ann and I talked about the confirmation that was now coming through. How could we possibly doubt spirit's contact with this world when two women had received separate messages that foretold the imminence of a breakthrough? It seemed to us that we were now in a time warp. Ann described this as a door being opened from the past. This symbolised the access to the akashic records.

But, she said, this door would only be open for a short period of time to allow the souls to communicate their secrets. Secrets were about to surface. Shortly afterwards, Ann brought out her tape recorder whilst we were travelling. She felt that some trance was coming through. What you are about to read is the full transcript of the recording from the other side. Certain words were inaudible and there will be dashes in place of the missing words.

*The pillow from his head is gone, **the bone fragments linger on**. In time they too shall be risen to release this young man from his prison. He's known the turmoil of the past ... He's known the hatred that's long last, but he wishes now to be free and in his place his trusty steed. He wasn't chosen, he was born to the manner of a king forlorn. His father **twice** did wish him dead, the nails did pierce his head. He was so sweet, he was so cold, he only wanted to grow old. Never a chance the sky to see, the crypt he lies buried beneath the sea. Men are born, men are bred, this dear sweet boy has left unsaid. For certain heartache he did cause—before—The past is past, the king's no more, the man's secreted behind the door. He waits in shadows, he bides his time, for he has got the golden line. He carries his messages far and wide. He will bring with him grim kings of tide. The king is dead, the king's no more, the king's in peace for sure. The past is past, the king is dead, the cushion's gone from beneath his head. But again will rise the golden dawn, never a care for words unsaid, always whispers at his bed. Whispers that begin to rise as proof the castle's full of lies.*

He cannot express the words divine to make this creature—His life was sad, his life was true, his life was fast. The king is dead, the king is dead, as it should be. His brother will reign quite supreme, the Cheshire cat has had the cream. We know no more of which to tell except to say—well—.

It is up to the reader to decipher the meaning of the above message. Ann said that the feeling she got was that Prince Eddy was resigned to the fact that his brother ('*. . . and in his place his trusty steed*') would take his place as the King.

It's important to point out that in both women's channelling there is mention of the Prince meeting his fate on the 'third' occasion. I have highlighted the words '*the bone fragments linger on*'. This is because Ann felt strongly that this was symbolic of a party game. '*His father twice did wish him dead*' appeared to be a dare to provoke the young Prince. It is known that his father would often deride him. Prince Eddy gingerly accepted this challenge on the third occasion. Was it Russian Roulette?

Ann Ann's automatic writing stated graphically what was about to happen when she wrote, '*The lid of the door is about to explode*'. Meanwhile, the other Ann's words were, '*Just open the akashic and all will come through*'.

The akashic records represent the secrets of the past, and this includes past lives. The ancient Egyptian god, Thoth, was scribe to the gods and he also kept the akashic records. Lord Ponsonby, Private Secretary to Queen Victoria, has been described as the 'great repository of royal secrets'. Ann's taped channelling (transcribed above) states, '. . . *the man's secreted behind the door. He waits in shadows, he bides his time, for he has got the golden line*'. Ann felt sure that the man secreted behind the door was Ponsonby. He was trusted by the Queen to deal with **all** communications including the most sensitive and secretive matters.

It was this web of secrecy that led to so many deliberate false trails which served to waste time and cover up many truths and indiscretions. These were to be found not only within the Royal Family, but also within the police and politicians of the day.

* * *

Today, we visited Stonehenge. Naturally, everyone was expecting to pick up some strong energy in this area. However, we were to be disappointed. But the day was not a total loss. As I walked with Christine towards the entrance of these ancient monoliths, she told me about a dream she had the previous night.

'I dreamt about the Prince last night. He was leaning over the body of one of the victims. And he was laughing. He threw gold coins at the women. But the dream was telling me that there was one time when one of the coins was different. He said it was his grandmother's Jubilee coin.' Subsequent research proved that coins were thrown around the feet of one of the victims, Annie Chapman.

Dreams are of great importance. They are windows to the past, future and our deep subconscious. They help us 'see' what we cannot in our normal, waking lives. Christine's dream contained enough detail to help us verify this particular incident. Detective work is done not only on the physical plane, but deep within the cavernous recesses of the mind.

The unsolved Ripper murders exemplify the manner in which important details were eliminated and suspicions diverted. But, secrets will always surface if more than one person knows about them.

20

Hush Hush

Looking back at the web of secrecy, Ann and I were trying to uncover some truths behind the Freemasons and their practices. Our own experience showed us how difficult it was at times to access records from the past. We were interested in Lord Randolph Churchill who was the highest Freemason in England, Magister Magistorum or Master of Masters, and the Prince of Wales who was a Grand Master of English Freemasons. We wanted to know if certain others were Freemasons and if so, when they were initiated.

We contacted the United Grand Lodge of England in November 1999. Their response was unhelpful. It was obvious that they did not wish to provide us with any details. We simply wanted to ensure that what was incorporated in the book was factual.

Some of the men we inquired about were Sir Charles Warren, Commissioner of the Metropolitan Police, London, and Frederick George Abberline who was also with the Metropolitan Police. We also needed confirmation on Sir Robert Anderson who was the Head of the Criminal Investigation Department in London from 1888. Sir Melville MacNaughten took over from Abberline, and we were naturally curious about his records. All of these men were connected to the Ripper murders and all were said to be Freemasons.

But, more significantly, there were two other men who held detailed information on the Royal Family. One was Lord Ponsonby, Private Secretary to Queen Victoria, and the other Sir William Gull, her Physician-in-Ordinary.

During the Ripper's reign of terror all of these men were in powerful positions. The murders continued after the main suspect's body was found in the River Thames. Montague John Druitt was believed to have committed suicide, and his body was found on 31 December 1888. The police then closed the case on the Ripper files as they decided that Druitt had killed himself after the alleged final Ripper murder.

Mary Kelly's body was found in Miller's Court on 8 November 1888. There is an interesting correlation here between a Freemason Lodge called the Quatuor Coronati and the death of the last victim. The Quatuor Coronati is a Catholic feast day and is celebrated on 8 November. Mary Kelly's body was found on 9 November. Also, Sir Charles Warren who was Commissioner of Police was the Master of the Quatuor Coronati.

It is important to highlight these details, because the case was not reopened when another Ripper murder took place the following year on 13 July 1889. Alice McKenzie fitted the profile of the other Ripper victims. She was 40 years old and her mutilated body was also found in Whitechapel. Only three weeks previously, the police ignored a letter allegedly signed by Jack the Ripper that stated, '. . . to resume operations in July'. By not reopening the case, the police effectively ruined the name of Montague John Druitt and his family. Druitt was used as a scapegoat to assist the police so that their cover ups and blunders could be concealed.

Another example of police cover up was the Cleveland Street scandal. It is interesting to note that at the height of the Ripper murders, Detective Inspector Abberline suddenly took charge of the Cleveland Street scandal in 1889.

The scandal involved young telegram boys, senior politicians and nobility. The venue was being used for homosexual activities. It is known that Prince Eddy frequented Cleveland Street. Why was Abberline appointed to both cases when others were available to perform this duty? And, why did it take Abberline six weeks to accumulate the evidence? Ultimately, this delay meant that the Cleveland Street culprits escaped their fate. Ironically, Abberline was congratulated for his efforts in this case.

Abberline was introduced to Robert Lees (a famous medium who regularly attended the court of Queen Victoria to pass on psychic information) who would help him with the Ripper case. Lees used his psychic abilities when picking up on the Ripper. On one occasion, he saw the Ripper donning a tweed coat to cover his bloodstained clothes. However, when he gave the information to Scotland Yard, his details were thrown out. The tweed coat that Lees saw suggests someone who had money. Unfortunately, Lees' offering was rejected and a murder took place that night.

Two weeks later, Lees felt that the Ripper was ready to strike again. That very night, two women were murdered. Perhaps the most chilling discovery he made was one that brought the police to the gates of Buckingham Palace. Lees claimed that the Ripper lived within these walls. Subsequently, Queen Victoria asked Lees and his wife to leave the country. They were paid for a year's stay in Switzerland.

Lees allegedly became a trusted friend of Detective Inspector Abberline, and their friendship extended to the famous medium becoming the Executor of his will. The question remains, why did Abberline gradually trust and respect this medium? The Detective Inspector was a Freemason, and he would have had an understanding and respect for ritual, and psychic manipulation. Is it possible that he found someone in Lees who could assist him in protecting and preventing the exposure of well-known colleagues? We can look back and see how this was effected during the Cleveland Street scandal.

Regarding the Ripper murders, the public was led to believe that there were only five women who were considered to be victims of Jack the Ripper.

However, when writing the book in Brisbane, Ann came to see me and said that she was getting another soul who had suffered six months before the first recorded Ripper killing of Martha Tabram. We then allowed spirit to show us where the proof could be found. Once we began searching, we found many more souls who had died in horrific circumstances.

These women were never humanised, and they need to be recognised as mothers, wives, lovers, sisters and friends. Yet, they were all described as 'prostitutes'. It is important to remember the old saying, 'There but for the grace of God go I'. Each was a victim of circumstance, and it is now important to bring one woman's story to your attention.

Emma Elizabeth Smith was a forty-five year old widowed mother of two. She displayed an incredible amount of courage and we feel compelled to share her story with you.

On 3 April 1888, Emma was attacked as she walked through Whitechapel. She lived long enough to report to police that she had been beaten, raped and stabbed with a blunt instrument. She also had an object obstructed in her vagina, which ripped the perineum.

To add further to this degradation and pain, the three or four attackers emptied her purse and left her dying in the street. Her determination and will to survive were incredible.

With horrendous injuries, she managed to stand up and wrap her shawl between her thighs to absorb the blood. She then made her way home where a lodger persuaded her that she needed to go to hospital. Emma Elizabeth Smith fell in to a coma and died soon after.

She was the first unrecorded victim of the Ripper era. Ann had picked up at the very beginning of the tour that there would have been more than one person involved in the killings. Here we found a situation where the victim managed to survive long enough to describe her attackers as three or four young men.

It is important to remember also that Ann had the feeling that there was a group of young men among the Freemasons who were separate from the older, established order. These privileged, young men were looking to go beyond existing limits, and to experiment with the more esoteric aspects of ritualistic power.

Was Emma Elizabeth Smith's description so accurate that it sent fear through the Establishment? Perhaps we can now understand why there was a need for the police to cover up important details. Were they familiar with Emma Smith's attackers? She could not have known the true identity of these young men. However, those who mixed in the same circles would have certainly recognised them.

Emma fitted the profile of a Ripper victim. She was in her mid-forties, and had to resort to prostitution in order to survive. Her reproductive organs had been mutilated, and the crime was committed in the early hours of the morning.

Following is a list of names that we found had suffered the same fate from February 1888 to February 1891:

Emma Elizabeth Smith, 3 April 1888, aged 45
Martha Tabram, 7 August 1888, aged 40
Mary Ann Nicholls, 31 August 1888, aged 42
Annie Chapman, 8 September 1888, aged 46
Catherine Eddowes, 30 September 1888,
  aged 46
Mary Ann Kelly, 9 November 1888, aged 24
Alice McKenzie, 13 July 1889, aged 40
Lidia Hart, 8 September 1889, age unknown
Frances Cole, 13 February 1891, age 26.

Possible Victims:
Annie Millwood, 25 February 1888, aged 38
Elizabeth Stride, 30 September 1888, aged 45
Elizabeth Jackson, June 1889, age unknown.

All these women were found murdered between midnight and 4:00am. The question now arises, how many others were there?

'*All their names will be cleared pure of sin.*' Ann's automatic writing now tells us clearly that these souls wanted closure and they are now free.

21

Death of a Prince— Birth of a Princess

Secrets from the past can no longer be covered up. It is time for the truth to emerge about the amount of suffering that young Prince Eddy had to endure. One doctor claimed there were signs of poisoning after his death. His nails had turned black, which is a sure sign of poisoning in the body.

Now, an important question must be raised. If opium was used to ease his pain at the time of the Prince's illness, was the family aware that his body was already laced with the concoction of strychnine and cocaine? This mixture was commonly used amongst the upper-class men with whom the

Prince socialised. If the family and doctors were unaware of this then they would have unwittingly hastened his demise.

As this was being written, Ann felt that the souls ranged from the poorest—just then Ann went into trance. It is important to give all the details of what she said.

'Get a pen and pad. All this blood, so much blood.' I ran off to get the pen and pad. Ann became deeply tranced. She brought her left hand to her mouth and looked out the window. I watched her eyes. She was in a state of fear and terror.

'So much blood all around me ... I can't seem to stop it. Can't seem to control it ... it's a miscarriage. Feeling all down that area ... a lot of anxiety ... don't want to lose it ... can't stop it. It's full term ... it's full term. It's a female. We don't know what to do ... they don't know what to do. They weren't prepared. Something dreadfully wrong. They're putting her in cotton wool and taking her away. The baby's in danger.'

I asked Ann, 'Who are you with?'

Ann told me she was in a big bed. I repeated my question, and she replied softly, 'Mama ...'

Ann's face was filled with horror. 'It's gone ... it's gone!'

I then asked Ann where they had taken the

baby. At that point Ann's expression changed completely. She was now more relaxed looking and turned around to look at me. She apologised, saying that she had gone in deeply and had felt a blockage before she went into trance. She knew that something had to be broken tonight, but didn't know it was to do with the young woman who had had a miscarriage.

'And I kept getting a name that began with an "E". It was either Ellene or Eleanor. But, that's the way it was pronounced. And I felt that although the baby looked full term, it wasn't really? It's just that the young woman seemed so immature . . . totally innocent. When she saw the child complete she thought that it was like a perfect, little doll. But, the contractions didn't feel like anything to me. It was a miscarriage.'

Ann told me that my question about where they had taken the baby acted as a trigger to pull her out of that scene.

'Suddenly, I felt so happy. I was having fun, and I didn't have the stress any longer. It felt as though it was about a year later. And mama was shopping for suitable gowns as we were going to the continent.'

It was late and Ann and I decided to stop for the night. We were aware that the infant was very significant in the telling of this story. Why did Ann tap in to this young woman and the traumatic loss of the baby at birth?

Ann had phoned me one morning and asked me to research Princess Helene of Orleans. She didn't know why, but she needed to know more about this young woman's background. I found out that when the Prince died, a beaded wreath with the name Helene arrived at Windsor chapel.

What is amazing is that it was left there on the instructions of Princess May of Teck. The Princess was effectively Helene's opposition in many ways. Yet, these two women found comfort together. Shortly after the Prince's funeral, Princess May urgently requested Helene to come and stay with her.

Furthermore, Pope-Hennessy's book, *Queen Mary*, provided me with an illuminating answer to Ann's question. I had a bookmark on the very page that talked of Prince Eddy's clandestine love affair with Princess Helene of Orleans. I explained to Ann that the reason she was getting the name Ellene or Eleanor in trance was because of the French pronunciation of Helene.

The couple had met in May 1890, and by August 1890 they were deeply in love and had asked Queen Victoria's permission to marry.

It is remarkable that in May 1890 when the Queen heard about the early stages of the relationship through 'her excellent family intelligence service, and her instinct like a Geiger-Counter', that she wrote to Prince Eddy saying he should not even consider marrying young Helene.

Yet, in August 1890 when the couple visited Queen Victoria to ask permission to marry (this was urged by Prince Eddy's mother, Princess Alexandra), the Queen feverishly began a round of communications to determine whether this marriage could be made possible. Why the change of heart, and why the urgency?

When I read about the chaos that was created by Queen Victoria and her band of merry men, it reminded me of the frenetic goings on at Sandringham surrounding the Prince's death. What is also remarkable is that during the Prince's delirium he had called out 'Helene! Helene!' whilst his fiancee, Princess May of Teck, was in the next room.

The problem surrounding the couple's relationship was that Princess Helene was a Roman Catholic, and this meant that she could not marry Prince Eddy.

'There now began a tortuous exchange of questionnaires involving . . .'

Pope-Hennessy's book went on to quote several names of those involved in communications regarding the matter. They included Queen Victoria, her son the Prince of Wales, the Prime Minister and the Lord Chancellor. The concern over the relationship between the French Princess and Prince Eddy was alarming. The Prince was willing to abdicate, and the young Princess personally visited the Pope in Rome begging his permission to marry. Why was there such urgency?

The answer, as it appeared to us, came through in Ann's trance that night. Princess Helene was pregnant. By April of 1891 the relationship had ended. The young Prince's line was never meant to continue. And the child born out of wedlock was never meant to survive.

The Prince died less than a year later. When the couple's relationship ended, Queen Victoria was told that Prince Eddy might never recover from this blow. And what of the baby who was whisked away in a carriage? Where was she buried? Where was the recognition of that innocent soul?

In his book, *Jack the Ripper: The Final Solution*, Stephen Knight has written that Prince Eddy fathered a child to Annie Elizabeth Crook. Crook supposedly had a daughter, but upon investigation no record could be found of marriage or birth.

However, the search encompassed 1884–1889. We discovered, through trance, that there was a baby born to Princess Helene and Prince Eddy.

The date was approximately December 1890 to early February 1891. This is a different time frame, and one that was not researched. Ann is positive that if research were undertaken it would prove fruitless.

There is an interesting piece of information in Knight's book, however, which backs up what Ann received through trance. Knight received a copy of a letter written by Mr Frederick Bratton to Lady Dowding. This letter contained an important and vital clue about the birth of a child fathered by Prince Eddy.

The letter stated,

'My grandmother was commanded to the court
to foster feed a child of the Duke of Clarence.'

Prince Eddy was given this title in 1890, the same year he was courting Princess Helene of Orleans. As far as the records show, Prince Eddy never fathered a child. The whispers of shame and secrecy have now turned to screams for recognition.

Ann and I talked afterwards, and Ann felt compelled to go back to our night in Strathpeffer when we all sat around in a circle in the dining room. That evening, we all shared what we were picking up intuitively on each other.

Ann had a feeling that Julie was a coach driver in a past life. She was in a very privileged position, because as a loyal and trusted servant, she held many secrets and could move around in the highest circles without question. Her total discretion also meant that she could be called upon to perform any activity requested by the Establishment. At the same time her peers would have equally accepted her.

Earlier in the book I mentioned that there was urgency around taking a baby away. Tonight confirmed Ann's feelings about that incident back in our Strathpeffer hotel. How can there be any doubt?

22

Ice Castles in the Air

27 October 1998

We were told on the tour that only one in every twenty-eight trips goes to Osborne House on the Isle of Wight. We were the lucky last for the season.

Whilst crossing the Isle of Wight Ann told me she kept getting 'Edes momma'. She explained that translated it meant 'Sweet mother, mother's milk or the true birth mother'.

This was fitting in with a quote I couldn't ignore from one of Shakespeare's plays.

'Were not I thine only nurse?'

In the play *Romeo and Juliet*, the servant who had wet-nursed Juliette had lost her own daughter. But this did not stop her from loving and caring for the highborn infant even though it was not hers.

I began to understand that my disappointment around Shakespeare's home had a lot to do with my expectations. I had felt that there would be a major discovery while we were there. This did not eventuate, but I could now see where Shakespeare's words fitted the puzzle.

Once again, I learned that every message has its place and time. Time is irrelevant in spiritual terms, but the messages should never be ignored simply because they don't fit in as and when we expect.

Ann and I began to wonder who was Prince Eddy's wet nurse? We didn't know what we were looking for. We would have to wait and see what spirit unfolded.

* * *

They say that patience is a virtue. But no one has told Ann this yet. She can become frustrated when things don't happen instantly! She has been known to demand that spirit, 'Get down here, and show me now!'

Queen Victoria's husband, Prince Albert Consort, designed the present Osborne House. The Royal Family enjoyed this hideaway as it was a place of retreat where they could relax away from prying eyes.

When we walked through the grounds, the weather worsened with both the wind and rain coming through. Ann could sense the feeling of freedom within the grounds.

'I can breathe,' she said. 'The correspondence would be of a written nature only. This meant that the Queen didn't have to deal with anyone in person.'

Nevertheless, this feeling of freedom soon changed to one of entrapment when we walked through the halls and rooms of Osborne House. Ann accidentally stood on the brass plaque where Queen Victoria's coffin lay in State. She said that it felt ice-cold.

'There's no warmth, no love and no grieving. It was time . . . it was finished. Because the era was finished . . . she was finished.'

The plaque is in the dining room where family portraits of the Royal Family hang. Ann asked the guide why the Prince of Wales was not in the painting. He then pointed out the Prince to her. The Prince was wearing a frock, as was customary for the first five years of childhood. After that, the young boys would dress in male attire. Ann wondered what effect this would have had on these young boys later in life.

We were then taken into a gallery where there were large, individual portraits of Queen Victoria and Prince Albert Consort. Ann is able to determine much about the character of someone from his or her picture.

'Queen Victoria would have been very petulant, and quite volatile. She would have been quite a handful.' Ann said that had she not been Queen, Victoria would have made a wonderful actress. 'And she was quite the martyr too.'

Prince Albert gave up his homeland and his friends, who were very dear to him, to become husband to the young Queen. He was only allowed one German servant, who became like a brother to him. He was his Secretary, Herr Doctor Schenck. The Prince could not have been prepared for what lay ahead within the marriage.

As Ann and I sat together to write this chapter, she became agitated and began to perspire. She got up to open the window for some air and said, 'Something's coming up. I don't know what it is. Just keep a pad and pen handy.'

Ann said she felt really angry and wanted to smash someone in the face. I was wondering how safe I would be! I wasn't all that familiar with trance, but I had never experienced anger through any of Ann's trancing.

'Victoria wants to come up.' Ann got a glass of

water and sat back down again. 'They're wanting to control the money ... too much spending. Queen Victoria wanted to live out her husband's dreams. She felt angry with him. He had all these grand ideas and when he died, he left her to handle it all. There was so much for her to do. And there was all this penny pinching. She hated her son. She believed he created havoc with his indiscretions. But, he didn't cause his father's death. The father also had indiscretions.'

Ann's face became dark and angry looking. 'For God's sake! Who do they think they are! I am the Queen. How dare they refuse this? I won't tolerate it. I will see them undermined. I'll make sure they never forget.'

Ann then spoke softly, 'Oh what a tangled web we weave ... tried so hard to keep it together ... but I can't. Albert said "Be careful. Don't let them know what your next step is. They want the Monarchy." What does he want? Does he want his pound of flesh?'

I was writing this down, but couldn't help noticing Ann was scratching the material of the sofa with her right hand. It seemed as though she was seething with anger.

'It will all go away. It will all go away.' Ann's voice was now light and soft. I was getting that she (the Queen) was living in 'la la' land. It would never go away. She wasn't living in the real world.

Ann then turned to face me. Her eyes were piercing, and her whole facial expression had changed. It looked cold and impenetrable. 'They can't implicate now.'

She continued to stare at me and I asked her, 'What can't they implicate?' Ann didn't answer. Once again, my question seemed to pull her out of the trance.

All the papers and documents, Ann said later, would show something. But they were burned. She explained that the feeling she got in trance was that there was not enough money. The Cabinet was concerned with the amount of money being spent. The budget needed to be controlled, but Prince Albert Consort and the Queen had no real concept of money. All of this was ammunition for the opposition. Looking back at the trance notes, it becomes clearer what was meant by Prince Albert's words when he said, 'They want the Monarchy.'

Queen Victoria had an enormous amount of anger. She expressed some of that anger outwardly when dealing with her husband, particularly about childbirth and sexuality, and public figures. But she repressed even more anger and confusion than anyone could have imagined.

Ann said that whilst she outwardly blamed her

son, the Prince of Wales, for his father's death, she knew in her heart that he was not responsible. There may have been a certain amount of guilt on the Queen's part, because she relied so heavily on her husband. Now she was angry because her husband had died and left her to cope. She expressed this anger towards her son because he didn't have his father's strength. And that meant he couldn't help her. She felt unable to cope. But in reality she was lazy. Ann began writing whilst I was typing. This is what came through about Prince Albert.

He was a man of sensitivity with a large streak of duty, born from what he not only felt but was instilled in his upbringing . . . to be a man, yet he was a servant. He was born to be king, but he became the man behind the throne.

Ann felt that Queen Victoria saw the Prince as a father figure. 'She wasn't comfortable with the sexual aspect of the marriage. I felt that she was hurt when he would go elsewhere for gratification. She wasn't hurt because of his actions, but because he was spending time away from her.'

We found a quote by the Queen which high-lighted her ambivalent attitude towards sex in a book written from the journals of Lord Edward Pelham-Clinton who was Master of the Household of Queen Victoria for over sixty years. 'Oh, doctor, can I have no more fun in bed?' This was after she had given birth to nine children. In what could have been a direct quote from Oscar Wilde, she once said, 'An ugly baby is a very nasty object and the prettiest is frightful.'

Ann felt very strongly that Prince Albert was a very sensual and sexual man. Queen Victoria wanted the romance and the attention, but not the physical intimacies. Yet, she was forced to endure the pain of childbirth. Her anger came from many levels.

Much has been said about the closeness of the couple. But it seemed that the relationship was based on her insecurities and fears. Ann became very animated. 'And, because Prince Albert would go with high class women, Victoria always had a fear that he may fall in love with one of them!'

The atmosphere in Osborne House was totally void of any warmth, if in fact any love or nurturing ever existed there in the first place. At one point during the tour of the house we found ourselves going in the wrong direction.

There is a rather eccentric need to have order and control within Osborne House. Everyone must move in the same direction and follow a specific route when viewing the property. We were so overwhelmed by the fact that it seemed more like a museum than a home that we ended up going the wrong way. We actually wanted to get out because I was feeling nauseous. I have visited a mental institution, and Osborne House had a smell that took me back many years to that asylum. It was not an antiseptic type of smell, but more to do with the sickness that came from the patients themselves. Ann felt that she was suffocating and simply had to get out and into the fresh air. But we were told that we had to go upstairs and see the rest of the house before we could leave!

This forced situation proved to be enlightening. Ann wanted to know the exact date of the young Prince's death. She didn't specifically say Prince Eddy, and this led the tour guide to provide information that surprised us. A young boy was born on 6 April 1871, and died on 7 April 1871. He was the grandson of Queen Victoria. The Prince and Princess of Wales lost their last child, but his name is barely mentioned in history. Why?

The time came for us to leave the Isle of Wight. The wind and rain had increased markedly. We were told that we might not get across on the last ferry. The previous ferry had been cancelled, and this meant that the number of passengers and vehicles had increased for this crossing. Fortunately, our bus was the last to be squeezed on to the ferry with barely an inch to spare.

The chop and froth of swell made it a very rough trip home. All other trips were cancelled for the day because of the inclement weather. Again, like the floods in Wales, we were happy to leave and continue our tour in safety. Always one step ahead of a natural disaster, it seemed that spirit had opened a door for a time and had given us the protection to complete this journey.

23

Messages From the Other Side

28 October 1998

Today was a day we had all been looking forward to for the duration of our trip. Before leaving Australia, Ann organised with the Spiritualist Association of Great Britain for our group to attend Belgrave Square in London to witness a demonstration of their psychic work.

This was to be a culmination of all our personal efforts because we had interacted as a group and given one another readings. Now we had the opportunity to see how these mediums worked.

It was to be a unique expression of spiritual communication. The clairvoyant who took the platform was a mature-aged gentleman who had the propensity to entertain the audience. He would choose someone from the crowd, and as he was giving the reading a psychic artist sketched a picture of the spirit who was coming through. On this occasion, the spirit was either a relative or friend who wished to get an important message through to someone on the earth plane.

The psychic artist sketched a female, and described her stature to add more depth to the reading. At the same time, the medium had chosen a young woman sitting at the back of the room.

'This is a relative. I'm getting your father's mother. Even though you didn't know her that well, she's here in spirit wanting to get a message through to help you ... She had a hard life, and she had difficulties with your father. In many ways, that's why you have a difficult relationship with him.'

The woman responded, saying that her grandmother had been a very strict woman. The medium said that it was important for the young woman to receive the strength that was coming through from her grandmother, and not to allow people to walk all over her.

This young woman had gone the other way and had become passive in the face of such strong, authoritarian influences. Spirit was telling her that she had an inner strength and could use it assertively. The granddaughter was living in fear of the father. Ann added to this saying that, 'She didn't want to be hated, she wanted to be loved. And she felt that being submissive would give peace. She didn't understand that this gave power to others to control her destiny.'

Ann and I stopped to discuss this. We saw where the mother dominated the son. In turn, the son was dominating the daughter. He felt empowered when dealing with her because she was his outlet for all the feelings of frustration from the past with his mother. He was never able to compete with her and did not want any other woman to control him in the same way. However, his daughter's destiny was to learn how to use her strength assertively and not aggressively as the father and grandmother had done in the past.

It made me think about Queen Victoria and her son, the Prince of Wales. The conflict and the jealousy between them cannot be ignored. He knew that she would never give up the throne despite the fact that, at times, she would have liked to be free of all the responsibility.

His frustration came from his inability to do anything about his situation. His mother held the power, and that was that. However, when the gentle, young Prince Eddy was growing up, his father treated him with the contempt he felt that he had been shown. In this way, he took advantage of his son's feminine characteristics.

Ann and I felt that the situation bore many similarities to the story of the young, passive woman and her domineering father. The grandmother in spirit is now trying to say she's sorry. She did what she thought was best, and can now see the hurt that has been created.

Queen Victoria was also someone who could only perform her duties within the strict parameters of her upbringing. Tolerance and compassion were qualities that she never fully embraced. But, once in the spirit world we do not judge. We see with clarity, and wish only to help those who reach out.

Earlier, I mentioned my belief that worlds do not collide—they blend. In this example, we can see how important it is to remain aware that spirit is constantly trying to help us from the other side. We do not walk the path alone. Each one of us has free will. But when we are helped, it is because of the power of this unconditional love. This love is so strong that it can transcend any earthly obstacle.

24

The Tower is Crumbling

29 October 1998

The last day of our tour. We were taken to London Tower and were told the history of the White Tower. This Tower was the original building and all the other buildings were added later.

There are seven ravens which fly around the Tower and never leave. This is because one wing has been clipped. The reason that these birds are 'Tower bound', legend has it, is that should the ravens ever fly away the Monarchy would crumble.

This began during the reign of King Charles II, when he was warned of the prophecy and thereafter he insisted that a small population always be kept around the Tower.

The ravens did in fact fly away during the bombing of London in the Second World War. It was the son of Lord Randolph Churchill, Sir Winston Churchill, who was determined to replace them. He was, like his father, a Freemason, but was initiated into the Druids in 1908. In Druidry, the raven is a sacred animal and it represents healing, initiation and protection.

The raven also describes the dark, destructive forces within us all. The destructive forces came during the Second World War when the enemy bombed the Tower. External forces, such as natural disasters which are nature's way of creating change, often lead to cleansing. However, Churchill feared change. His fear came from the dark, destructive forces within him. These forces were enough to motivate him to replace the ravens to ensure the continuation of the Monarchy. Was this powerful, political man so superstitious that he feared going against his occult beliefs? Ann's feelings were that the Monarchy began crumbling when Queen Victoria died on Tuesday, 26 January 1901. No longer was the country's matriarch able to control events. The ruling power, as it is today, was with a woman.

Today, there are two males who are next in line for the throne. When we look back at the male heirs who reigned in Britain, we can see that their positions were short lived. And the reason for their abrupt endings within the Monarchy was, it would appear, because of a woman.

The yeoman at the Tower also told us how King Charles' astronomer complained about the mess that the ravens had made on the end of his telescope. He was unable to see through the lens and asked that the ravens be removed. But, so great was the King's fear of the prophecy that he removed the astronomer instead, sending him to another building.

As I listened to this story it immediately struck me how another astronomer, Galileo, had his vision imprisoned by power and authority. He was a man with a vision, and someone who discovered a truth that neither the church nor the authorities wanted to hear.

Galileo presented the hierarchy with the news that the earth was not the centre of the universe, but that the earth and all the other planets revolved around the sun. This was a revelation and was not well received by those in power. They feared what this 'heresy' might mean to them and their positions of power. The Inquisition was brought in and Galileo was placed under house arrest. Unable to express his true findings, he gradually lost sight in both eyes. There is a fascinating parallel between Galileo in Europe and King Charles II in England.

King Charles II took the throne in 1630, and Galileo had just finished writing his work concerning the 'Two World Systems'. Power and struggle, truth and denial seemed to echo throughout the world simultaneously.

We were to experience a similar era on our last night in London. Previous arrangements had been made by the tour company for us to attend a medi-aeval banquet. We were taken to a restaurant under the Thames. A dark, cavernous place, I wrote in my journal how frightened a person would be if they didn't know the area.

Everything was set up to reflect Tudor times. The theme of Old England carried through to the names of the tables where people sat. We were led to the Tower table! And so we had come full circle. Ron was selected from our group to be king, with Linda as his queen. They were given robes and crowns to wear to further colour the atmosphere of the evening.

At the end of the evening, Jimmy Ruffin's 'What Becomes of the Broken Hearted' was playing and I felt compelled to record a few significant lines of the chorus. Everything we had received was being reinforced down to the table we dined at on our last night. We had been told of Traitor's Gate, which was a secret passageway used by smugglers until the 1600s. However, it was interesting that the guide told Ann that Traitor's Gate was later used for the convicts when they were sent to the colonies in the 1800s. It was clear that it could be used when necessary.

When the evening finished, Ann and I decided to go back to her room to gather all the paperwork associated with her automatic writings as the others were to fly back to Australia the following day, and I was going on to family in Scotland.

During our discussion in the hotel room I decided to switch on the tape recorder. Ann was saying that she couldn't shake the feeling that there was a murder about six months before the first known Ripper victim. She said that the enjoyment was there.

'I keep getting the feeling . . . the man going into the Tower archway . . . that takes you down to the water. That's how he got away.'

Then I heard her voice drop, and I realised that she had slipped into trance. What you are about to read is a transcript taken from that night's recording.

Quick! Quick! The master's waiting . . . smells fishy. Not fish . . . oil . . . work . . . he rubs something in. He does dirty work for someone. I feel he ate cheese and bread. The Prince wasn't in on it, but he was in on it. This killing's not as clean ... he's getting scarred. I feel around the jaw line.

Ann's voice becomes lighter and she slips into trance another time.

Going away to the countryside! Not strong, not well ... croup or flu. They won't stop watching me ... always at me. I can write. I can write my own things if I want to! Why don't you leave me alone? I hear what they're saying. I don't care. [Then, in a soft voice] Oh! Mama would be so proud!

'Sorry, I have to come out.' Ann then told me what it felt like whilst in trance. She talked of the scrawny man who was calling out, 'The master's waiting.' She described him saying that he looked older than his years.

'He looked about fifty-five or sixty, but when I felt his hands they were of a man in his forties. Maybe this was the effect of the oil ... I don't know.'

In another scene, she saw him sitting at a newly

scrubbed wooden table. It was in a sandstone basement, which sounded to me like the servants' working quarters of that era. As I wrote this, Ann said she could hear the sound of horses' hooves on the cobblestones outside. 'And there's a plump woman who seems to be in charge of the others. She's waiting on him.'

She saw cheese and bread on the table. There was also a gold ring. It wasn't a bracelet, but it was too large to be a finger ring. It had some fine engraving on it. Later, Ann realised that it was a serviette ring.

So, this man was in a privileged position amongst the servants and they acknowledged his position. It would be in their best interests to give him what he wanted, because they believed he had the ear of the master. Little did the servants know just how much the master despised him. The gold ring was a status symbol for him, because he felt this made him superior to the servants. Yet, Ann felt that he had no scruples and that his work was of a suspect nature. He did anything for a price.

Ann then explained how she felt as the Prince whilst in trance. 'I went out of town, somewhere nice ... country area ... had a hospital type feel. I was in an open carriage, you know, with two seats on either side. Dark ... plain ... no insignia. Other members of the family have been there.'

She didn't know why, but she kept getting 'Jock'. She said, 'I don't know what that's about?'

I explained that Jock was a Scottish nickname, and was also used for a Scotsman living outside his country. Ann then said that she felt the Ripper victims were selected on the criteria that they would not be missed. Also, one or two were chloroformed and a dentist or someone with dental knowledge had administered this. During this explanation, Ann was desperately trying not to slip into trance again. The reason being that she knew I had not experienced someone going into trance on my own before.

She continued, 'They were sacrificed for an experiment. But, someone *enjoyed* it. That's when it got out of control.'

Looking back on the trance material we realised how important John Netley, the coach driver, was to the Ripper murders. During our research, we found an excerpt from *Jack the Ripper: The Final Solution*, which talked of John Netley's alleged involvement with the Ripper cases.

> 'He regularly picked up Eddy from a pre-arranged spot.'

In this context, Stephen Knight was referring to the Prince and his supposed love affair with Annie

Crook. Whilst this is not what Ann was picking up, it still highlights that Netley was central to the secret rendezvous that took place. Further, it states that Eddy would transfer from the Royal Coach to Netley's carriage to outwit any 'prying eyes' of Royal Aides.

* * *

Ann received a letter from Julie two years after the tour. She wanted to let Ann know that she thought, '*it was a great idea to show how we bring characteristics into our present life from our past lives . . . I'm happy for you to do this with my life*'. What followed was automatic writing that Julie channelled on 18 September 2000 which contains remarkable similarities to the story of the coach driver John Netley.

> *The major answers to all the questions I don't feel can be consolidated to a concise form as you would be to persist in writing them. However, the most eventful thing . . . your contribution in the event was to seek out and destroy any evidence. The reason why no one heard anything or saw anything was because you were able to make it so. Your position in the Queen's Guard allowed you autonomy to*

move throughout many areas, always concealing anything which could ever result in a link to your subject. The clairvoyance you were given was so you knew you were there. It was on those same pebbles you stood waiting. They are looking for the lost links, which you hold and most of the things in this life are clues as to what happened in the past. Sometimes things aren't always what you believe to be correct. But it is with great care ... you need to trust others to be correct. The waiting and not knowing drove you mad. Frustration would build up ... the waiting on Tower corner to ensure the safe return of your subject notoriously cut deep into your sense of justice. Your love of animals comes from a deep understanding of knowing where you are. They are never anything but what they are ... they don't pretend to be something they are not. You are relaxed in their presence, calm in their honesty. The constant effect of keeping people living within a preordained idea of what they are leaves you resentful of human nature. And it's these things which frustrate you still in smaller ways, but not enough to be noticeable, people covering up the deceit and deception. The special treatment which is given to some and not to others. Differentiation by wealth ... The accolades taken but the work not done, and the worst of all, dealings completely out of your control. Having to do things, not because you feel them right, but because you are obligated.

Your work is one, which again swears you to secrecy knowing what is going on, in a way, but not entirely. But again perpetuating the false sense of what is real that people are living. I hold the real story, and allow them the finances to perpetuate the illusion they are living.

My work is now looking for, and locating deceit and deception.

I was an old, nearly retired man ... the coachman ... no one wants to see what is right in front of your face, hence the ease with which one can then hide it. Nothing at the time was so different to now, except people persisted in looking in the wrong direction. Why we were all brought together, was to find common ground from which we could all then follow new paths by reliving those traumatic experiences *which we have all brought into this life-time. We need to heal in order to continue. What we shared once brought us all back together. Because, only together could we find the links between what we suffer now and those initial sufferings. My life still favours the security and faithfulness and honesty of animals. They do what is asked of them and there is no falseness about them. They are what they are. Good luck with the book . . .*

Ann and I felt it was important to include the full letter. Julie crossed two boundaries within her automatic writing. She talked of her past life, then discussed her present situation. This is not uncommon when our past holds the key to resolving an emotional problem in this lifetime.

When Julie wrote about waiting for her 'subject' at 'Tower corner', I thought that she might have been repeating what Ann channelled on the last night of the tour in our London hotel. But, we didn't speak to the others after that night, and Julie was unaware of the information Ann had channelled that night.

* * *

John Netley seemed to be an insignificant pawn in the game that was being played. But it was too hard for us to ignore how significant he really was. He was chosen for his lack of conscience. He would do anything to rub shoulders with anyone of influence. This involved taking part in homosexual activities, which he really did not enjoy. For all his efforts, his death merely reflected the gruesome life he led. John Netley was run over by his own carriage on 26 September 1903.

Ann felt strongly that the Ripper murders revolved around experimentation and ritual.

'Two messy ones, two amateurish ones. One was a twin murder ... two identical done by the one person. I'll give you six killings ... Didn't stop that quickly ... more than one person involved. Three people ... six killings. They had to prove individually that they could do something. The problem came later when someone had the taste for the kill, and couldn't stop. It was no longer an experiment. It was fun. It was power!'

It was Dr Thomas Stowell who, in 1970, suggested that Prince Eddy was the killer. Soon after this, the Royal records claimed that Prince Eddy could not have been within the vicinity of the murders, because he was staying with friends or family. However, they quote four occasions only. There were more than four murders. In addition to this, he was recorded as staying for several days at each location. There could have been times when he took off, and no one would have dared questioned his absence.

25

'The Picture of Prince Eddy'

P rince Eddy enjoyed socialising with the liter-ary and artistic set. Amongst his friends were the artist Walter Sickert and writer Oscar Wilde. Earlier, I mentioned the interest both Ann and I had in Oscar Wilde. This is where a parallel story can be told.

Wilde wrote *The Picture of Dorian Gray* in 1890. It tells the story of a beautiful young man who never wanted to grow old. Prince Eddy never did grow old, and when Ann first intuitively chose the book from the library shelf, she had no idea how enlightening the tale would be.

Wilde must surely have struggled with his

conscience because the book clearly reflects his need to express the truth about the gruesome nature of events around him at that time. These events not only included his knowledge of the Ripper murders, but also the experimentation that was going on within his peer group.

In the past, it was difficult to truly express the meaning behind one's art. And any works that involved taboo subjects had to be dealt with discreetly. To be published, a writer would need to conform to moral codes of the day.

Here, in Wilde's book, it is impossible to ignore the inference of homosexuality. He did in fact take a great risk when writing this story. His soul needed to express his truth. As an observer of the tragedies of indulgence that surrounded him, he felt compelled to write about what he knew.

It does not take a great stretch of the imagination to liken Dorian Gray to Prince Eddy. Once again, we are not suggesting that Prince Eddy was the murderer, but that his life of escapism led him to some dark situations where his peer group would encourage him to participate in murderous rituals of the Ripper era. Like Dorian Gray, his beauty and status drew others to him. Here the Prince found a life that not only excited him, but also made him feel accepted.

On Dorian Gray, Wilde said, 'all excess, as well

as all renunciation, brings its own punishment.' These words reverberated strongly one evening when Ann and I were listening once more to the tape where she was channelling Prince Eddy. This is when he had been taken away to the country to recuperate. Ann had something more to add.

'I hear what they're saying, but I don't care. "You've got to remember your position." I don't care. "Have a bath! Have a bath!" I don't want to. They want me to keep clean.'

The Prince had contracted syphilis at the age of sixteen whilst on a tour of duty on HMS *Bacchante*. Afterwards, Ann said that she felt the Prince was sick of trying to keep clean. It would never work. His personal staff thought that the discharge he was suffering was due to masturbation. In fact, it was because his syphilis was getting worse and the discharge wouldn't go away.

'And, I'm feeling pain around the back passage. Could it be crabs? It's as though he was suffering all the time from both areas. I felt he would literally go mad from the burning, stinging sensations. He wanted to ease his pain, and he couldn't even get the berry juice? I don't know why I'm saying that?'

Ann eventually realised that the 'berry juice' was an alternative treatment for his condition. The Prince felt that it would be the cure, but he knew that it could only come from someone who specialised in this area.

'Think of your position . . .' Ann said that she felt this was his equerry telling him how dangerous it could be to chase after this alternative cure. The equerry argued with him because he feared that the Queen might find out about this through Sir William Gull, her Physician-in-Ordinary. Gull specialised in the treatment of syphilis. Ann began picking up on Gull and felt that he would not be averse to passing such information on to the Queen if he thought it was in her best interests. Prince Eddy respected his equerry's opinion on this matter.

Still picking up on the Prince after listening to the tape, Ann felt that the Prince had a lover within the palace.

'I'm feeling as though I've just come home, and I'm flopping down in a high backed chair, throwing my right leg over the arm of the chair. And these boots I have on are beautiful . . . they're dark leather. I've got a red jacket on with gold braiding, and the buttons are open. But, there's nothing underneath. And I'm anticipating sex. Oral sex. I'm looking forward to the enjoyment of this man. He's my lover.'

Ann believed that the lover was his equerry. Prince Eddy's equerry was the brother of Frank

Miles, the artist. Frank Miles was at one time a lover of Oscar Wilde.

One only has to read the first two pages of chapter two in the *Picture of Dorian Gray*, to see that the author is expressing the theme of homosexuality. The inclusion of Dorian's lover, Sibyl Vane, appears as a token female within the story. However, she does represent an important character within the Ripper murders. When Ann first read about the death of Sibyl Vane in the novel, she felt sure that this was a connection to the first Ripper crime.

In the book, Vane is a young actress who kills herself. She was deeply in love with Gray, but he tired of her. Her brother, a policeman, vows revenge for his sister's death and wants to kill Dorian Gray whom he believed maligned her and was the cause of her suicide. He eventually is shot during a hunting mishap. Dorian Gray is relieved because now he knows that his pursuer cannot identify him. He is no longer threatened.

Ann read this immediately as being the first Ripper attack. Looking back on the files, there was a young policeman who had detailed knowledge of several murders. He was getting close. She said that he either nearly caught the Prince in the act, or he did in fact apprehend him. But the police cover up meant that the young man's life would

have been in danger, although he was unaware of
this. He found it difficult to accept that he had to
turn a blind eye. However, his fate was sealed. He
was stabbed to death in Whitechapel trying to stop
a brawl.

The Prince clearly had close encounters when
on his escapades. It is important to repeat Ann's
automatic writing from 29 October 1998.

> 'He came from a place beyond the trees,
> he was not alone ... all about him was
> quiet. He knew he could be seen at any
> time, but that did not distract him from the
> purpose at hand. His quest was quite clear,
> get the job done and then relinquish his
> fear.
>
> The power of the soul is not to pass on
> without at least seeing how the other one
> lived. Thus you will see into the future.
> Enjoy the kill; receive the rewards
> ... regret is not for now but for later. He
> walked away with his head held high;
> those in the know sang praise. Little did
> they fear the outcome that would be, the
> pigs in the wood would see clear. They
> came so close to catching him, but he
> alone was not guilty of sin. The clan were
> proud for in their wake was the future

219

*king that could create, he bore his soul
and they gave the score.'*

The above writing does not need an explanation.
But there is a quote from Wilde's novel that ties
in with the disappearances of the Prince on these
nocturnal adventures and the introduction of
another wild card in the Prince's life.

'Sometimes when he was down at his great
house in Nottinghamshire, entertaining the
fashionable young men of his own rank who
were his chief companions, and astounding the
country by the wanton luxury and gorgeous
splendour of his mode of life, he would suddenly
leave his guests to rush back to town to see
that the door had not been tampered with, and
that the picture was still there.'

This is a section of Wilde's novel where Dorian
Gray is anxious to see the portrait of himself
painted by an artist called Basil Hallward. Each
time he returns to look at the painting he sees that
his image has grown older. When Gray invites the
artist into his room to show him that the painting
has taken on a life of its own, Hallward is horrified
by the eerie and hideous transformation.

In real life, Walter Sickert was an artist and close

friend of Oscar Wilde, and as mentioned earlier he introduced Prince Eddy into their social circle. Sickert claimed that in a half conscious state he had sketched the Ripper murders. Stories abound of how Sickert had helped the Prince and Annie Crook with their clandestine meetings. He also accused many people of being involved in the Ripper murders such as Sir William Gull.

Yet, Ann felt strongly that it was the wild card, Sickert, who had a heavy hand in pushing the boundaries and daring the other young men to do the same. His paintings reflect a drug-induced state. The danger of this man was that he was able to instigate any wild games, and the other young men would follow him. They were unaware just how removed this man was from reality, and they themselves ended up in a similar frame of mind. Everything was out of control and going too far.

What began as a painting of beauty and innocence in *The Picture of Dorian Gray* was to later turn into the reflection of a man's tortured soul. A man who had gone too far. That man was Walter Sickert.

Oscar Wilde could not have known that this book would become the prophecy of his own demise. He describes a man who had to flee his own country because of accusations and scandal. Ultimately, *The Picture of Dorian Gray* was considered too offensive, and Wilde later integrated six more chapters which diluted the effect of the novel and appeased those who were shocked by the content. Wilde was forced to do this because any form of writing was better than no writing at all. If he were unable to write, he would have lost the will to live. Wilde was sent to prison for his truth.

Earlier I wrote of Galileo's frustrated efforts to express his vision. He was not permitted to declare what he knew. Subsequently, he lost his vision. Galileo was placed under house arrest for daring to tell his truth.

Both Wilde and Galileo knew that they could do no more than maintain their integrity within the parameters that society allowed. Their deepest beliefs led to their incarceration. I feel that the following quote from Shakespeare's King Henry VIII sums up perfectly the lives of these men. Just before his death, Cardinal Wolsey says, *'I feel within a peace beyond all earthly dignities'*.

26

The Ravens Have Flown

'There is talk he was Jack the Ripper you know.' And so, Princess May of Teck lost her fiance, but she gained a life as Queen Mary. How would her life have unfolded had she married Prince Eddy? As it turned out her life was dedicated to the survival of the Monarchy. But, like Queen Victoria, Queen Mary was happiest when she was away from her Royal duties.

Ann feels this is reflected in the present day Monarchy. Prince Charles is at his most relaxed when he is able to enjoy nature, for he has a very deep spiritual awareness. Yet, as with those before him, his life was not destined to be a happy one. He lost the mother of his children, Lady Diana, and now he is not permitted to marry the love of his life, Camilla Parker-Bowles. Added to this, he has waited in the wings for a part that he will never be destined to play.

How much longer will it be before the Monarchy realises that it does not hold the same power it once did? Yes, the ravens have flown, and the Tower has collapsed. Like the Druids who revered the Goddess because of her power, the Royal Family has always been 'dominated' in one way or another by its women. The men of the Royal Family have not faired so well during their reign. Whether that is through abdication (as with Mrs Wallace Simpson and King Edward VIII) or through a woman ruling is of no consequence. For example, King Edward VIII was left with an uneasy feeling on the day of his father's death when the crown's Maltese cross fell from the coffin and into the gutter. The King wrote, 'Although I'm not superstitious, I wonder whether it was a bad omen'. Within a year he would no longer be King. The fact remains that, directly or indirectly, women have had control of the Monarchy's destiny.

At the beginning of our journey in London, we stayed at the Tower Hotel and Ann and I discussed the meaning of the Tower in tarot. It is the only image that is man-made. It represents a façade.

And, when the Tower is struck by lightning, as is shown in the card, the structure crumbles. All false values must now be faced. All truth must now be exposed. This is enlightenment.

On the last night of our journey, we travelled by coach to the airport. I suddenly had a feeling to turn around and look behind me. There, in the night sky, was a beautiful display of fireworks. No matter what turn we took on the road, the fireworks followed us. It was clear. Spirit was saying, 'Thank you'. The souls are now free.

27

The Riddle of the Rose

26 December 2000

I had a fitful sleep last night. The strong ocean breeze made the cedar wood blinds clatter against the window frames. Eventually, I drifted into a deep slumber. That's when the dream began.

I'm out on the ocean, standing on a narrow concrete island. It reminds me of the Pacific Ocean in North America, because the light is softer than the harsh West Australian daylight that is familiar to me. It filters through the grey sky and textures the small, peaked waves. It is not stormy. There is no swell. All around me men are treading water in the calm of this scene. There is silence. I look up at the sky and see an enormous black cloud in the distance. Streaks of black rain form under the amorphous shape. I am transfixed. I know what is about to happen. The cloud does not evaporate, but instead crashes down onto the ocean with great speed. It hits the water as if it is a solid, concrete mass, and at the same time I hear an enormous thunderclap like some angry God who must be appeased. The light is beginning to dim because of the surrounding clouds. I turn around and see another cloud quite close to me. It is about to hurtle down in the same way as the previous one. But this time I fear that it might hurt me in some way. I become disoriented and have to remain calm or I will fall into the ocean and all will be lost. There is only one man left in the water, and I know he is trying to be brave and ignore the enormity of the situation. But I also know that man cannot fight the elements, and this man is at the mercy of the elements. He cannot help himself or me. All I can do is remain calm. The second cloud crashes into the water with the same ferocious speed and sound. I'm still standing. The soft, grey light is

returning. I turn around and see two beau-
tiful images in the distance. Two ocean
liners sail towards me. Their presence is
powerful, and they are there to help.

But even more beautiful and unusual
than this, is another image on the ocean
between the ships and me. I am looking at
a white stallion with its front legs raised,
and its rider is an eighteenth century mili-
tary man. He is fearless and the horse is
powerful. I run along the narrow concrete
island and I am bursting with excitement.
Not because I am about to be saved, but
because something is about to be revealed
to me. My quest for knowledge is about to
commence. A mystery is being unlocked.

I woke up feeling exhausted. This is familiar to
me. When spirit works through me I often feel this
way after a dream. I have paid attention to my
dreams ever since I was a young girl when my
mother used to ask me what I had dreamt about
the night before. I would tell her, and she would
explain the dream to me. I always knew if the
dream was symbolic or prophetic. On this occasion, I felt that it was a mixture of both. Spirit
speaks to us through the world of dreams and I
was sure that there was an important message for

me in my dream of Christmas night. I wanted to know what it was about.

Later that morning, I decided to relax and watch one of the videos I had picked up just before Christmas, a documentary on the *Titanic*. There was footage of elderly passengers who had been interviewed many years after the event. I couldn't understand why I was still so interested in the *Titanic*, especially as I had just sent off the final manuscript of the book to the publisher. Yet, there was something niggling deep within me that would not rest.

At the end of the documentary I saw an internet address which I noted. I became discouraged however, when I couldn't access the website, and was just about to give up when I noticed a piece of paper next to my computer. It only had a few words on it: 'The Riddle of the Rose, by W.B.M. Ferguson.' Then I remembered that it was my intention to follow this clue.

Christine, who was part of the psychic tour, had unearthed this information in one of the book-shops that we visited. The reason behind Christine's discovery went back to the beginning of the trip. We were in Trinity Church when Ann said that she saw a beautiful red rose. She wasn't sure of its significance, but was sure that something would eventually be revealed. Christine dutifully pursued the meaning of the red rose throughout the trip, and when she stumbled on a book entitled *The Riddle of the Rose*, she was keen to let me know about it. I really did not want to let Christine down, because she had made a special effort to help us, so I began my search on the internet hoping that it wasn't too late to add my findings to the book before it went to print.

Again, I met with disappointment. Finally, after several attempts, I found a book called *The Riddle of the Rose*, but it was by an author called Lynn Brock. What came next both surprised and excited me. Lynn Brock was one of a few pseudonyms used by the author. I was shocked when I discovered the author's real name.

But, before revealing the author's name it is important to remind the reader of the earlier chapter where Ann and I discussed the possibility of a cover up around the true events of the *Titanic* disaster. I mentioned that Ann had written down the name 'Alister' who was somehow connected to the *Titanic*. I also mentioned a dream I had about sitting an exam where I had to answer certain questions. My feeling was that I knew the answers, only to find out later that I was incorrect and someone else in my dream (an old colleague of mine) had all the details, which somehow negated my responses. The old colleague, who I knew in real life, was called McAlister. Ann felt that my dream had to do with a cover up at one of the *Titanic* inquiries.

With this knowledge in mind, I was amazed to discover that the author's real name was Alister McAllister. I was further intrigued to read that McAllister served in the British Intelligence. He was also a Chief Clerk at the National University of Ireland and had written numerous, complex crime fiction novels and plays. An author will often use a pseudonym to avoid detection of sensitive political or personal matters. This was discussed earlier when I wrote of Oscar Wilde's life.

There was another interesting fact I discovered about McAllister's life. Apart from working for British Intelligence, he worked in Ireland where the *Titanic* was built. He was born in 1877 and died in 1943. The *Titanic* sank in 1912. McAllister would have been thirty-five years of age. This was his era. I had to phone Ann and tell her of my discovery. She had no doubts about the connection.

'And the funny thing is,' she laughed, 'I got the video of the film 'Titanic' to watch at Christmas.'

It appeared to me that the dream I'd had was urging me to pursue the mystery of the *Titanic*, because there was more help on its way. Ann and

I both agreed that the information would be best placed as a postscript to the book, because more information would surely unfold in the next one. The following day, Ann followed up some more information about McAllister and she told me that he had written *The Riddle of the Roost* and not the *The Riddle of the Rose* as was quoted on the internet.

'It really doesn't matter,' I said. 'We've been led to this in an abstract way, and it's exactly the sort of 'riddle' or red-herring that McAllister may have enjoyed sidetracking people with in his crime novels.'

As I spoke to Ann I sensed that she wasn't her usual self and asked if there was anything wrong. She revealed that she had not slept properly for quite some time, and that strong emotions were beginning to surface. Oddly enough, Ann had been coming into my thoughts a lot recently and I wondered why. She felt that psychically, she was ready to close down. All the work that she had been doing over the last few years since her cancer surgery meant that physically, she had reached breaking point and she needed some time off to rest. She had helped me through a very difficult time in my life, and it was connected to this book. I now felt strongly that Ann needed help to bring to the surface whatever it was that was troubling her. My feeling was that she too had something to release with this story. And it seemed as though it was just about to be revealed at the end of the book. Or could it be that something would unravel with the next book? I was puzzled, but felt compelled to pursue this. There is one quality that Ann and I both share. Tenacity.

28

Final Note

It is hoped that the reader will recognise the many so-called coincidences that took place to help unravel the mysteries of the past. One or two coincidences can be ignored, but when there are so many unfolding we can be sure that they are more than just 'coincidence'. This is when spirit is hard at work trying to help us understand how we can work together to heal our lives on this earthly plane, and recognise the importance of past life experiences. We are human, and we do live in the 'real' world, but that world needs to be opened up so that all limitations and barriers are removed.

This story has ended, but there is another one to follow. Ann said she felt that a survivor from the *Titanic* had passed something on to a family member. This could be anything from a story or a letter to a piece of jewellery. The relative has perhaps forgotten about the incident. However, *Death of a Prince* will jog their memory and they will come forward. This connection will be vital to our next book.

There is often a strong pull by spirit to get a message through to a loving relative. They may want to help resolve something, and then move on. Spirit will cross all boundaries to reach that person. At times, there may be great distances to span, and this is when the media can help. A book, a radio programme or television can be an extraordinary tool of communication.

* * *

Alison's Story

The following story is an example of how one such incident occurred. One weekend, Ann kept seeing a little girl who had long, white-blonde hair and wearing a green checked uniform spinning around at the bottom of her garden. This was a spirit child called Alison. She told Ann, 'I'm free, I'm free!' Ann was unable to help unless Alison gave her more information. The little girl said she would be thirteen years and nine months now.

At the time, Ann was doing both a local and national radio programme. It was on Tuesday night when Ann was doing the national radio programme that she saw the little girl again. She was able to see her reflection in the glass, and once again Alison was happy and spinning around.

Ann knew immediately that she had to get the information out on air. Someone had to know who she was, so Ann told the listeners about Alison and that she felt she had passed over when she was about five years old. The following letter arrived at the studio two weeks later.

FINAL NOTE

Mrs Lynnette Adams

Dear Anne,

On the 5th November 96 on your show you said a spirit had been in to visit you. You said she was a young girl, in school uniform with long blonde hair, who died young, named Alison and would now be 13 or 14. I tried for 1½ hrs on the 5th and all of the show on the 12th to call you.

But I decided to send a photo of my second daughter.
Name: Alison Louise Hamilton
Age died: 5 yrs 9 mths
With: cystic fibrosis
Last photo: in her green checked school uniform
Would now be 13 yrs 7 mths.

Was it her who made contact with you and are there any messages?

* * *

Thank you for whatever you see for us and may god be with you and much bright light fall upon you.

With regards,

Lynnette Adams

Ann then called Lynnette, who was living in central New South Wales, on air. Lynnette said that she felt the little spirit child was her daughter. She told Ann that she had been asking an angel to let her know if her daughter was free from the crippling cystic fibrosis now that she was on the other side.

Ann then said, 'She's telling me to tell you to go to the biggest tree.' At this point, Lynnette became very emotional. Finally, Ann asked her what it meant. Lynnette explained, 'I'm known in the area for hugging trees.'

* * *

To all those who took part in the journey thank you. You all had a part to play in this unique experience. We wish to offer special congratulations to Christine. Christine was the young woman who, when we were in Wales, slipped into trance and described her life as a nurse whose wishes were thwarted when she wanted to help the soldiers during wartime. During the trip, she had talked of her desire to become a nurse, but didn't feel she would be able to cope with the exams. Although she was a gentle soul she had steely determination. Ann received a letter from her with a Christmas card in 1999. Christine passed her PCA nursing course with flying colours.

References

Albert Victor, Duke of Clarence and Avondale, 1864–1892, *The Cruise of Her Majesty's Ship 'BACCHANTE', 1879–1882* (London: MacMillan & Co, 1886).

Aronson, Theo, *Prince Eddy and the Homosexual Underworld* (London: John Murray (Publishers) Ltd, 1994).

Coren, Michael, *Conan Doyle* (London: Bloomsbury Publishing Plc, 1995).

Dewar, James, *The Unlocked Secret: Freemasonry Examined* (London: Corgi Books, 1990).

Dyer, Colin, *The History of the first 100 years of Quatuor Coronati Lodge No. 2076*.

Ellmann, Richard, *Oscar Wilde* (London: Penguin Books Ltd, 1987).

Fisher, Graham and Fisher, Heather, *The Queen's Family* (London: W.H. Allen & Co Ltd, 1982).

Fisher, Trevor, *Scandal: The Sexual Politics of Late Victorian Britain* (Stroud: Allan Sutton Books, 1995).

Harrison, Shirley, *The Diary of Jack the Ripper* (London: Smith Gryphon Ltd, 1993).

Harwood, Gwen, *Selected Poems* (Sydney: Angus & Robertson, 1975).

Hyde, H. Montgomery, *Lord Alfred Douglas: A Biography* (London: Methuen Books, 1984).

Kinloch-Cooke, Sir Clement, *A Memoir of Princess Mary Adelaide, Duchess of Teck* (London: John Murray, 1900).

Knight, Stephen, *Jack the Ripper: The Final Solution* (London: George C Harrap & Co Ltd, 1976).

Nevill, Barry St John (ed), *Life at the Court of Queen Victoria, 1861–1901* (Exeter: Webb & Bower, 1984).

Pope-Hennessy, James, *Queen Mary, 1867–1953* (London: George Allen & Unwin Ltd, 1959).

Short, Martin, *Inside the Brotherhood: Further Secrets of the Freemasons* (London: Grafton Books, 1989).

Wilde, Oscar, *The Picture of Dorian Gray* (Harmondsworth: Penguin Books, 1949).

Wilson, Colin and Odell, Robin, *Jack the Ripper: Summing Up and Verdict* (London: Bantam Press, 1987).

Woodham–Smith, Cecil, *Queen Victoria: Her Life and Times, Vol. 1, 1819–1861* (London: Hamish Hamilton Books, 1972).